GROWING UP
IN THE KIBBUTZ

*Comparison of the personality of children
brought up in the Kibbutz and of
family-reared children*

GROWING UP
IN THE KIBBUTZ

By

A. I. RABIN, Ph. D.

Professor of Psychology,
Michigan State University

SPRINGER PUBLISHING COMPANY, INC.   **NEW YORK**

Copyright © 1965

SPRINGER PUBLISHING COMPANY, INC.
200 Park Avenue South
New York, N.Y. 10003

Library of Congress Catalog Card Number: 65-25096

Type set by CAROL-GUINN, INC., New York
Printed in U.S.A.

Preface

Relatively few accounts of the development of children in the Kibbutz are available in the professional literature. Most of these accounts are descriptive, episodic and impressionistic; some of them are second-hand reports that have led to misconceptions concerning the child rearing process and the product of this process in the Kibbutz. Furthermore, authors have found it difficult to divorce their descriptions and interpretations of the behavior of Kibbutz-reared children and adults from their theoretical and ethnocentric biases.

The purpose of this volume is to present a systematic account of child rearing and education in the Kibbutz, and a systematic exploration and interpretation of the personalities of Kibbutz children at several age levels—from infancy to maturity. Moreover, this is a *comparative* study in which the Kibbutz child is assessed alongside the Israeli child born and reared in the conventional family setting. Thus, the Kibbutz child is not compared with the norms of Western society (which explicitly or implicitly have been employed by various observers) but with those of representatives of the broader culture which he shares.

The book consists of three parts. The first part (Chapters 1-3) sets forth a fairly detailed description of Kibbutz child rearing and education and, on the basis of current theory and available research, raises a number of questions regarding the effect of these antecedent conditions. The second part (Chapters 4-8) presents the procedures of assessment and the methods of investigation employed, as well as the findings obtained with these operations. For four age levels, group comparisons of Kibbutz and parallel non-Kibbutz children, on a number of personality dimensions, are summarized, discussed and interpreted. In the last part of the volume (Chapters 9 and 10) the author attempts an integration of the findings—what the Kibbutz child's personality is like, and how it differs from that of the child reared in the nuclear family setting. The relevance of the findings to theory and their implications for child rearing and education in general are also included.

Psychologists, psychiatrists, social workers and others in the helping professions may find this book useful in gaining some perspective regarding the universality of principles we hold dear and immutable, but which, possibly, are culture-bound.

Cultural anthropologists may be interested in a psychologist's venture into the cross-cultural domain—exploiting the natural "laboratory" conditions provided by societies different from our own.

Educators will be interested in the results and implications of the "collective education" movement, unique and viable in its sixth decade of existence.

No work of this nature can be accomplished by one person, without the cooperation of many other individuals. It is a pleasure to acknowledge the help of many friends and colleagues, here and abroad.

I am most grateful to the late Shmuel ("Milek") Golan, pioneer educator and theoretician of the "collective education" movement whose personal interest, cooperation and stimulating conversations, as well as his writings (Golan, 1960), have greatly aided me in carrying out this project. Other leaders of Kibbutz education—Mordechai Segal, Gideon Levin, Ada Hagari and Menahem Gerson—have greatly facilitated the process of data collection. There are many others—teachers, metaplot and parents—too numerous to mention, without whose help my task would have been impossible. Thanks are also due to Dr. Gina Ortar, of the Hebrew University, and to Eliezer Garni and Daniel Eliram, Majors of the Israeli Army. The assistance of my former colleagues and students in the United States, especially in rating the responses of the several tests, is also gratefully acknowledged. Drs. Mary Haworth, Joshua Levy, Paul Berg and Jacques Levy have been very helpful in performing these tasks at various stages of the project.

A Sabbatical leave of absence from Michigan State University made it possible for me to spend nearly the entire calendar year of 1955 in Israel. An additional eight months in Israel, in 1962, were permitted by another Sabbatical and assisted by a grant from the International Programs-Ford Foundation, at Michigan State University. I am very grateful to the University and the International Programs for these opportunities afforded me.

A. I. RABIN

New York City
June 1965

Contents

Contents

Acknowledgements

Some of the tables in this volume are based entirely or in part on previous publications by the author.

Tables 5-2 and 6-3 are drawn from data reported in Tables 3 and 4, respectively, in the *American Journal of Orthopsychiatry*, 1958, *28*, p. 581. Table 6-10 is based on Table 5, *American Journal of Orthopsychiatry*, 1959, *29*, p. 177. Table 7-1 appeared as part of Table 5 in the *American Journal of Orthopsychiatry*, 1964, *34*, p. 498. Table 6-5 is drawn from Table I, *Journal of Projective Techniques*, 1957, *21*, p. 151. Also, Tables 6-6, 6-7 and 6-8 appeared in the same journal (1958, 22, p. 331) as Tables I, II and III respectively.

For permission to use these tables, acknowledgements are gratefully made to the *American Journal of Orthopsychiatry* and the *Journal of Projective Techniques*.

1.

Introduction

The phenomenon of the Israeli Kibbutz is not altogether unknown to the well-informed reader. A number of brief as well as detailed descriptions of the economic, social and educational structure of the Kibbutz have been published and widely read. In recent years, especially since the establishment of the State of Israel, acquaintance with this type of unusual society has broadened and deepened. To many, however, it will come as a surprise that the beginnings of this type of collective settlement in Israel date back to 1910—more than a half a century ago (Baratz, 1955).

Essentially the Kibbutz is a voluntary organization. Persons who established this type of settlement were not forced to do so by any central regime, as is the case in the communist countries at the present time; nor was their motive solely economic, as is the case in China, the USSR, and in several of the satellite countries. The people who banded together to establish the Kibbutz did so from personal conviction and belief in the justice of economic collectivism and social equality. They were idealists. From their various backgrounds, especially Russia and Eastern Europe, these immigrants culled an ideal for their future life in the new country. The Kibbutz represented an embodiment and realization of the cherished ideal.

1

Entirely voluntarily, groups of people, in the country then known as Palestine, established small agricultural settlements based on the principle of economic collectivism and social equality. Private property was confined to a very few personal possessions. All else was collectively owned. The means of production belonged to the community as a whole, as did the returns from the economic enterprise. Each person was to be given according to his needs, with no opportunity to rise above his fellows financially or economically. All needs—shelter, clothing, food, entertainment—were to be handled by the community.

In addition to, and as a consequence of this economic equality, social equality was the ideal. Equality of status for different occupations, for the sexes, and for persons of varying productive capacity was the rule.

During the past fifty years the Kibbutz movement has grown considerably. From the small beginnings in 1910, some two hundred and thirty collective settlements have sprung up throughout the country. Waves of immigration from Russia and Eastern Europe in the 20's 30's and 40's, supplemented by mounting immigration from such Western countries as Germany, Austria, and Czechoslovakia and Hungary in the late 30's and 40's, have supplied the Kibbutz movement with many additional recruits. A sizable percentage of these newcomers had been trained in youth movements whose major mission was the preparation of the young for Kibbutz life in Israel. Here the emissaries of the Kibbutz movement transmitted the ideals and tenets of its founders to thousands of youth clamoring for immigration and the establishment of a life based on social and economic justice and equality.

During and following World War II, the youth movement atrophied. The entire Jewish community in Europe was mangled and massacred, and the "raw material" for the Kibbutz movement in Israel all but disappeared. The 1950's saw a meager growth of the Kibbutz movement, and very few new Kibbutzim (plural of Kibbutz) were established. Most of the recruits came from the older Kibbutzim themselves and from the native Israeli youth movements. The new waves of immigration, chiefly from Oriental and Near

Eastern Countries, did not contain the human material which was ready ideologically or psychologically to embark upon an adventure of collective living.

At present, the 230 existing Kibbutzim containing a population close to 100,000 persons have lapsed into a comparatively static state. Their relative percentage in the country's population is decreasing, and their influence in the country as a whole is waning.

Ever since its inception, the Kibbutz movement has enjoyed considerable status and prestige. Not only was its membership made up of hardworking, idealistic intellectuals, but their role in the defense of the country was outstanding. They were looked up to as pioneers capable of great endurance, persistence, and of an unswerving devotion to the realization of their ideals—social, national, as well as moral. The Kibbutz movement, because of the nature of its manpower, supplied leadership for some of the major parties in the country as well as in the administration of the new state. Even today some half a dozen ministers of the Israeli cabinet are members of Kibbutzim. The Prime Minister himself has become a member of a relatively new Kibbutz in the South (Negev), to which he retreats occasionally from the cares of government.

Politics are taken seriously in Israel. Belonging to a political party—instead of merely registering and voting occasionally during elections—involves quite often a passionate adherence to an ideology, to a *Weltanschauung*. Labor parties predominate, ranging from the religious right to the communist left. There are three major labor parties. *Mapai* (Labor party of Israel) is by far the most influential party. It is social-democratic in its platform and has been the largest party in the State since its founding. *Achdut Ha'avoda* (Unity of Labor), is a bit to the left of Mapai, but eschews communism. *Mapam* (United Labor party) is far to the left, definitely Marxist in philosophy, but maintains a considerable nationalistic ideology to keep it away from international communism.

The Kibbutz movement is very politically conscious, but not of uniform political persuasion. Because of historical circumstances and because the political parties maintain different educational youth movements, three major alliances, or federations, of Kibbut-

3

zim have been established and are in existence to date. They pledge their allegiance to the three labor parties.

1. The *Ichud* (Union) federation is primarily affiliated politically with the largest labor party, Mapai.

2. The federation called *Hakibbutz Ham'uchad* (The United Kibbutz) is composed chiefly of members who belong to Achdut Ha'avoda.

3. *Hakibbutz Ha'artzi* (National Kibbutz) is an amalgamation of Kibbutzim whose membership form the backbone and provide the leadership for the leftist labor party, Mapam.

Aside from political and ideological collectivism, these federations guide and govern the economic, cultural and educational life of the Kibbutzim that constitute their membership. There is a good deal of federation-wide planning in the fields of marketing produce, buying goods, constructing agricultural and industrial enterprises, in cultural activities (including publishing establishments), and in education and child rearing. Each federation maintains a central educational bureau, located in the major city of Tel-Aviv, which reviews educational policies and child rearing practices, and proposes changes and modifications which are ordinarily binding to settlements that are members in the federation. Thus, in the Kibbutzim there is a certain uniformity of educational practices and programs, consonant with the decisions of the federation's educational bureau, which by and large represents the overwhelming majority of the membership.

With respect to educational practices and child rearing, the federations differ in degree of centralization. The Kibbutz Artzi manifests the highest extent of centralization; the Ichud, probably the least. As a consequence, a good deal more diffuse experimentation takes place in the Ichud than in the Kibbutz Artzi or the Kibbutz M'uchad. This distinction served as a major reason for concentrating our study in Kibbutzim which are members of the latter two federations.

Speaking of uniformity in practices is not to deny, however, a certain individuality and local atmosphere which may color the operations within any one settlement. We are persuaded, though,

4

that these are not major factors or modifiers of the personality variables with which we shall be concerned in this book.

THE KIBBUTZ SOCIETY

Utopian communities of the past, in Europe and in the United States, were isolated little islands within a hostile, or at least indifferent, larger community and culture. They were tolerated as a "lunatic fringe" or as wide-eyed idealists whose social experiment is sooner or later doomed to failure. These utopian communities were, in a sense, escape movements; they negated the *status quo*. They were too few and too weak to exert any influence on the "outside" community and did not represent any political force in their countries. This is not to deny, perhaps, the moral influence of these communities through their ethical standards and values.

The Kibbutz movement is in many respects different from these ventures in centuries past. The difference accounts for the greater viability and vitality of the Israeli Kibbutzim. Although for the founders negation of the *status quo* as it existed in the countries from which they came was a strong motivation, the comparatively large number of people in the Kibbutzim, their social and political sophistication and the educational programs directed to the preparation of the youth have been a force of considerable impact on the State of Israel. They do not represent escapism but a sort of hard-headed idealism. They have proved themselves economically, militarily and culturally. The individual Kibbutz is far from being an island utopia. It is not isolated ideologically, for it maintains membership in a larger federation of like-minded communities. The Kibbutz movement as a whole constitutes a sub-culture within a larger, more diversified culture with which the points of contact and influence are quite numerous.

The typical Kibbutz has a membership of some 200 adults. The total population of the village is usually around 500, including children and some special immigrant training groups. A number of Kibbutzim, however, especially in the Kibbutz M'uchad federation, have populations of well upward of 1000 souls.

5

As a part of the general background of our study, several of the more important Kibbutz institutions require mention in some detail.

The Kibbutz is a fairly complex democratic organization in which most of the important decisions regarding any phase of its life are rendered through the town meeting type of instrumentality or *Sicha K'lalit* (general discussion). These meetings of the entire adult membership of the Kibbutz take place one evening weekly; sometimes more often. Not only are current issues, pertaining to the economic, social, cultural and educational life of the village, dealt with and decided upon; long range planning and election of various committees and functionaries also take place at the town meetings. Standing committees on village economy, planning, work assignment, education, security, etc. are elected annually; also elected at the town meeting are several important officials who centralize and coordinate the activities of the committees and the Kibbutz as a whole. Some of the major positions, which often require full time engagement on the part of the persons involved, are those of the manager of the economy, the treasurer, the Kibbutz secretary, who also chairs the town meetings and maintains liaison with the federation to which the Kibbutz belongs, and the "work assigner" who is the chairman of a work assignment committee and is responsible for the daily division of labor in the entire organization.

As far as the several economic and service branches are concerned, each is headed by a sort of "foreman" who is responsible for the particular branch, who is its "manager." The word for the position is "merakez" which means the one who centralizes or coordinates. There are "managers" of the poultry branch, the vegetable gardens, orchards, dairy, central kitchen and dining room, etc. These people actually do the work themselves, often with the aid of other members, depending on the work demands of the job.

Occupational specialization in the Kibbutzim has not been great. The majority of the members shift from one branch to the other, depending upon the need of the economy. Often, specialists in one branch are "plugged" into another branch. One Kibbutz member commented: "We all have to be the 'plugs' at one time or another." All members take turns at such chores as dishwashing and serving in the central dining room.

The dining room in the Kibbutz is the focus of its activities, the central place for contacts between the members of the community. Since individual families are not involved in housekeeping and in preparation of meals (except for occasional light snacks), all adult members of the Kibbutz meet at least three times a day for their meals in the dining room. (The children eat in their own dining rooms, as will be described in detail in Chapter 2). The general meetings, parties, celebration of holidays and a variety of cultural events take place in the dining room. The work schedule for each day appears here the evening before on a special board. The dining room is often in the physical center of the Kibbutz.

The most crucial aspect of Kibbutz society for the present study is the unique nature of the family within the Kibbutz structure. The "family" in the Kibbutz does not meet most of the major criteria assigned by sociologists to this institution. Families in the Kibbutz cannot be defined as functional economic units, nor is the socialization and control of the children a prerogative of the family. These facts reflect a basic ideological principle of Kibbutz philosophy, "the liberation of the women and the children." This objective reflects the rebellion of the founders of the Kibbutzim against the *status quo*, against the conventional society and family which they viewed with profound dissatisfaction.

The "liberation of the woman" expresses itself in regarding women as equals to men in rights and responsibilities. Women are not to be dominated by their husbands. They have equal rights in Kibbutz society, and married women often keep their maiden names as a symbol of not becoming the "property" of the husband. In conversation, Kibbutz members do not ordinarily refer to another member by his last name. However, when there are two or more members with the same first name, they are referred to as the one belonging to so-and-so (the spouse). For example: "David shel Miriam," i.e., Miriam's David, distinguishing him from another

7

David, and vice versa: "Miriam shel David," when his wife is referred to.

Married couples live in individual living units consisting sometimes of a single room with no indoor toilet facilities; this may be the case in younger, less affluent Kibbutzim. In the older, well-established Kibbutzim, the living quarters often consist of small apartments of one or two rooms, with private toilet, porch, etc. Kitchens are not included in the design of these living units, for the central dining room serves all the major meals of the day. However, most couples have a hot plate on which they often prepare "four o'clock tea" (or coffee) or late evening snacks. Preparation of these informal meals is not the duty of either husband or wife. They often alternate or work jointly. The food supply, obtained ordinarily from the dining room, is quite minimal. A large item is that of goodies for the children when they come for their daily visit.

Part of the emancipation of the woman is also expressed in her being freed from the chores involved in child rearing. The children are brought up in separate "children's houses" where they are cared for by professional workers. Their daily contacts with either parent are limited to an hour or two, after working hours. (Details regarding this specific arrangement follow in the next chapter.) The founders of the Kibbutzim and especially the ideologists of Kibbutz education saw in this schema of living the "liberation of the child." The child no longer has to be the victim of a tyrannical father or doting, neurotic mother within a patriarchal type of family organization. The child is not to be dependent economically or psychologically, upon his biological parents, thus avoiding a feeling of debt and possible guilt and rebellion. The entire Kibbutz as a sort of "extended famliy," is replacing the nuclear family unit.

RESUME

As a backdrop against which we will describe our investigations, we sketched briefly the main features of the type of Israeli community known as Kibbutz. The first Kibbutz was founded over 50 years ago. The Kibbutz movement to date has 230 units or settlements, divided into three major federations, with a total population of close to 100,000 persons.

The main principles of the Kibbutz are economic collectivism and social equality. It is a voluntary organization composed of like-minded individuals attempting to realize economic and social justice. It is a democratic organization in which all full-fledged adult members participate.

The entire Kibbutz rather than the family, as we know it in Western society, is the important unit. The economic and child rearing functions of the traditional family have been transferred to the Kibbutz as a whole. Parents have both limited control of, and responsibility to, their biological children. It is this unique process of child rearing and education in the Kibbutz which is the main concern of this work. A description of this process appears in the next chapter.

2.

Child Rearing and Education

Shortly before delivery, the expectant Kibbutz mother is taken to the central or regional hospital, which is part of the network of medical services maintained by the vast labor union federation in Israel. Several days following delivery, mother and infant return "home"—to the Kibbutz. The mother returns to her own quarters which she shares with her husband, while the infant is placed in the "infant house." Henceforward the child is, with rare and exceptional interruptions, in the company of his peers until he graduates from the *Mosad* (institute), or high school, at the age of eighteen, when he becomes eligible for adult membership in the Kibbutz. As we shall see, the separation from the parents is only partial. The infant and child rearing process passes through several stages which we shall describe in some detail.

INFANTS

A. The infant house—physical arrangements

Ordinarily the infant house is equipped to accommodate 18-20 children from the first week of life to about 15 months. The building is made up of two separate sections—one section for the very young and another for those who have been weaned. The younger babies

10

are placed in two large rooms, five to six in each room. Besides, this section contains a workroom (including a refrigerator and a stove for heating food), a dressing room for mothers, toilets, and two large porches used at different times of the day for placing beds or playpens. In each of the large rooms there is also a corner for bathing and caring for the physical needs of the child. Every infant has his own crib and toys. In the room there are also chairs for mothers who breastfeed their babies.

The section for the older infants (those who were weaned) also accommodates six children in a room with a corner for the necessary "services" (heating food, folding laundry, etc.). There is also a room for crawling and playing. A porch with a separate entrance is used for placing playpens with two to three children in each. These playpens for the older infants are much larger than those of the younger ones and offer ample opportunity for crawling, trying to walk, and for other ventures in exercising newly acquired mastery and coordination.

The Kibbutz usually attempts to make these houses as attractive as possible. The walls are painted in appealing colors, and are often adorned with pictures, curtains and flowers. An attempt is also made to place the house in attractive physical surroundings.

B. Early care of the infants

Just as child rearing practices have changed with the years in other countries and societies, so in the Kibbutz. Kibbutz educators have constantly kept their ears cocked to the "latest" pronouncements and interpretations of research findings concerning the process of child rearing. The description of present procedures does not hold for years past, just as present child rearing practices in many Western countries bear little resemblance to those in vogue during previous decades.

During the past decade the Kibbutz mother has become involved, much more deeply than in previous years, in infant care, feeding and general close contact. Demand feeding is the rule in the Kibbutz. Thus, during the first six weeks of the life of the infant, the mother is available whenever needed. Breastfeeding is en-

11

couraged. Mothers, however, who do not breastfeed also take care of all the feedings during the first six weeks following confinement. They do not have to return to work during that period.

After the first six weeks, a feeding rhythm is established and the mother feeds the infant at about four hour intervals—five times a day. The feeding itself lasts about 20 minutes, but the time of contact is usually extended to about 45 minutes or an hour. Besides feeding, the mother also changes the diapers during that hour, carries the infant, plays with it, and finally puts it to sleep. In some instances the mother may be permitted to sleep in the infant house for several weeks, especially when late night-feeding becomes necessary. Ordinarily, however, the self-demand schedule is established for the hours of the day. Occasionally, when the child wakes in the middle of the night, the night watchwoman may give him something to drink and pacify him. Only in exceptional cases the mother is wakened so that she can come and attend to the infant's needs.

After the infant is six weeks old, the mother resumes working on a half time basis until he reaches about four months of age. During that period she continues her breastfeeding (or bottle feeding) and caring for the infant during several periods of the day. After the infant is four months old and the mother has returned to full time work, the number of feedings is gradually reduced and the child is "weaned"—is given the bottle and solid foods—by the time he is five to six months old. This is a very gradual process, and the timing may differ from individual to individual. The mother continues to have the major part in the care of the infant until he is about nine months old. The evening feeding and putting the child to bed is still the mother's prerogative until he is about a year old.

C. Role of the metapelet

The literal meaning of the word *metapelet* (plural: *metaplot*) is "the one who takes care" of the child—the nurse. The metapelet is in charge of the infant house and its inhabitants. She is responsible for the house, its order and cleanliness. She also follows, carefully, the health of the child, washes him and bathes him, takes care of any additional food he requires, weighs him regularly, and serves as liaison with the physician who makes his visits from time to time. She keeps close watch over the infants when the mothers are not around, and keeps notes concerning the behavior and any special reactions of the children. She also guides the younger and inexperienced mothers in the process of feeding and taking care of the infants during their period of contact.

The metapelet is available to the child when he cries or is restless; she comforts him and plays with him in the absence of the mother. She does this increasingly as the infant gets older and the time of contact between mother and child decreases. Ordinarily there is one metapelet for every five to six children. During the period of earliest infancy, the metapelet may have charge of a larger number of infants since the mothers do a good deal of the work involved.

When the infant is about six to nine months old, his group (of four to six infants) gets a "regular" (permanent) metapelet who stays with the group for approximately the following four to five years—through the toddler stage until, and sometimes after, they enter the kindergarten.

The regular metapelet of infants in the second half of their first year is with the children from morning until the middle of the afternoon, about 2:00 P.M. Her assistant is there when the children waken from the afternoon nap, around 3:00 o'clock. She picks the children up, dresses them, gives them their milk, and plays with them until the parents come to pick them up for the daily visit with them, from about 4:30 to 6:30 in the evening. Then, when the parents return the infants to their house, the regular metapelet is back again, feeds the children, undresses and bathes them, and puts them to bed.

D. Contacts with the family

In addition to the contacts that the biological mother maintains with her infant during the early months, there are also some contacts with the other parent and with the biological siblings. Weather permitting, the family may take out the infant for a short visit (one half hour) when he reaches three months of age. During the latter part of the first year of life the length of the visit may extend to as much as two hours. In addition to the parents, the siblings of the infant are also present during those visits. Visiting is after the regular working hours of the parents. They are, therefore, during that period, completely "at the service" of their children.

Parents' or siblings' visits to the infant house are usually not encouraged, except when they pick up the child or return him. Unexpected or irregular visiting tends to upset the routine of the children as well as of the metapelet, who usually has her hands full.

THE TODDLERS

A. The toddlers house—physical arrangements

As mentioned above, the infant house keeps children until they are about 12 or 15 months old. After that period each group of infants (of five to six children) is transferred, *as a group,* to the toddlers house. Ideally, Kibbutz planners advocate a toddlers house for two groups of six children each, divided in two units. However, in reality the physical arrangements differ. Many toddlers houses are larger and include more children and more units.

The house in which the toddlers remain for approximately three years, is equipped to meet their needs and development. Aside from bedrooms (often, still four to six children per room), service areas and porches, the houses have playrooms with many toys—for the increasing activities of the toddlers. A dining room is also included.

Another feature of the toddlers houses is the play yard surrounding them or adjacent to the porches. The yards are enclosed, but within them there is freedom of activity; they contain a sandbox, simple "jungle gym" equipment, and other materials appropriate for the small groups of toddlers.

B. Care and supervision—the metapelet

The regular metapelet who took over the care of the group of infants during the last several months in the infant house accompanies the group when it is transferred to the toddlers house. The role of the mother in caring for the infant had already become considerably reduced during the latter part of the first year of his life. In the toddlers house, the metapelet "takes over" fully and literally. She is responsible for the rearing of the toddlers in her group. The responsibility is entirely and completely hers.

Training in self-feeding and eating habits, toilet training and other habits of cleanliness are directly handled by the metapelet. She helps the child learn how to dress and undress and get ready for bed. She supervises the play of the children. When they are around three years of age, group play is introduced for short periods. Here the metapelet aids in the transition from the individual, spontaneous play to more organized and cooperative types of activity. In addition, she takes the children for short walks, leads them in exercise and rhythmic games, teaches them songs and tells them stories.

The metapelet is with the children most of the day. The exception is the "visiting period" when the children go or are taken to the parents' quarters, after work, for a couple of hours daily and for longer periods on Saturdays and holidays.

C. Contacts with the family

The pattern of family contacts established at the beginning of the toddler period is followed through the Kibbutz child's eighteenth year, after which he begins to be considered an adult, enters the Army, and becomes a full-fledged Kibbutz member. As mentioned above, official contacts with the parents and siblings are confined to the two to three hours of daily visits with the family, following work hours (late afternoon and early evening). After the visit, the toddler is usually returned to his house by his parents. The daily parade of parents returning children to their houses about 6:30 or 7:00 in the evening is a familiar sight in every Kibbutz.

Upon their return to their house, the toddlers are met by the metapelet, who has in the meantime returned from her own quarters and, probably, from a visit with her own children. She feeds the children and then puts them to bed. In some Kibbutzim (especially in those of the Kibbutz M'uchad federation), the parents put the children to bed. This procedure is sometimes quite a trial for child-

15

ren and parents alike. Imagine several children and several pairs of parents, crowded in one bedroom, trying to put them to bed, to say goodnight to them, tell them stories, sing songs, and engage in a variety of other quieting methods. In many instances the separation for the night is quite difficult and becomes expressed in temper tantrums, "new games" and a variety of other subterfuge on the part of the children.

After the children are put to bed, the duties of the metapelet are over until the following morning. The night watchwoman takes over until morning. Usually she makes the rounds to different children's houses—infants to preadolescents. Her job is not an easy one, for a great many problems need to be faced and dealt with. In one house, a child may waken and start crying; soon he may be joined by the members of his group in a wailing chorus. In another house, a child may suddenly fall ill, feel pains, or need a drink or some reassurance about his fears, nightmares or anxieties. The watchwoman usually attempts to pacify the children, reassure them and comfort them. This is not always effective, and one or more children of a group may spend a sleepless night. Further discussion of the role of the night metapelet and possible implications of still another figure in *locus parenti* will be postponed until later in this, and in the next chapter.

THE KINDERGARTEN

Generally the children remain in the toddlers house through their fourth year of life and somewhat beyond. At age four to five they become members of the peer group known as the kindergarten. Whereas the groups during the infant and toddler period were small (not more than six children), the new grouping, in the kindergarten, consists of about 18 children—combining three groups transferred from the toddlers house.

The Kibbutz concept of the kindergarten is different from the conventional one. The kindergarten stage covers a period of about three to four years and includes the equivalent of first grade school work. Thus, the child remains a member of the kindergarten until approximately age seven. Upon leaving the kindergarten, the children become second graders.

A. Physical arrangements

The kindergarten is housed in a building of its own; the building contains bedrooms, a play and work room, a dining room, showers and toilets, as well as porches and a large yard around it. The yard is equipped with suitable articles for gymnastics and different types of play and recreation. Some work tools are available. Small gardens and enclosures for animals are also provided.

A reduction of the number of children per bedroom takes place at this stage. About three to four children in each bedroom is the usual arrangement. The bedrooms also have special "corners" for toys and books so that the child has an opportunity to follow his own interests beyond the group activities of the kindergarten. The group activities are part of the formal program, but time is allowed for informal individual and spontaneous play as well.

B. The personnel and the program

Personnel for the 18-child kindergarten consists of a teacher and two metaplot. Thus, the ratio of children per metapelet increases from 6:1 to 9:1, approximately. The metaplot get assistance from less regular workers with some of the household chores and during some necessary absences and weekends.

Most of the morning, the children in the kindergarten are in the charge of the teacher whose function it is to conduct group activities and help each individual child develop his creative potential to a maximum. A short period in the afternoon is set aside for formal, organized activity. The number of hours under the direction of the teacher increases with the years that the children spend in the kindergarten.

Federation and Kibbutz educational authorities have worked out in detail an organized and methodical program designed to develop the physical (muscular coordination) and sensory (including musical and visual-artistic) capacities of the children. Art, music and "rhythmics" are important, especially in the early period of

17

the kindergarten curriculum. In addition, nature study, with emphasis upon the flora and fauna of the vicinity, is emphasized. During the summer season (which lasts eight to nine months), the children take frequent walks and "hikes" in order to get acquainted with the area surrounding the Kibbutz. Many of these experiences are coordinated and related to each other so that they lead up to the "project" system which dominates the teaching of the school which the children will enter later. Essentially, a progressive educational approach dominates the program.

During the kindergarten period, the children also begin to get acquainted with the Kibbutz workaday world. The teacher takes them on tours of the various branches of the Kibbutz economy; they visit fields and the gardens, stables and chicken coops, packing houses and small factories. These visits serve as topics for prolonged discussion of the group with the teacher, who explains and who answers the numerous questions. At this time the children begin "working" themselves. In addition to taking care of the small garden outside their building and of the small animals which they may keep nearby, the children make their own beds, set the table at meal time, and do a few additional small chores as part of the day's routine.

The last year, before entering the second grade, is called the "transition kindergarten." The children, usually in their seventh year of life, are now taught the fundamentals of the three R's in group and classroom instruction. But they still receive a good deal of individual attention. An attempt is often made to help a particular child in acquiring these skills—according to the level of his maturity and development. Since "outside" teachers are rarely employed in the Kibbutz, the teachers who are also members of the Kibbutz are expected (and are available) to spend longer hours with their pupils than is customary in the conventional school systems.

During this last year in kindergarten, there is an increased emphasis on group activities in every area, on mutual aid, discipline and, generally, on greater social interaction and integration.

C. Contacts with the family

In discussing the toddlers, we have indicated that the pattern of visits and visiting time to the parents' quarters, established during that period, is maintained throughout childhood. In the parents' room there are usually "corners" or closets for each child, containing some toys that are the child's "very own." The child is not expected to share them with anyone else. If there are several children in the family, each has a corner with his "personal" belongings, suitable to his age level and interests.

During visiting hours it is not an unfamiliar picture to see each child turn to his corner and check on his belongings, play with them, and try to draw one or both parents into his activities. This is especially true with the younger children—the older toddlers and those in kindergarten. Expressions of sibling rivalry and competition for the attention of the parents during the visiting period are not altogether uncommon, especially when the siblings are close to each other in age.

Toward the end of the kindergarten period, as the children get more involved in group activities, their visits in the parents' quarters become spontaneously shortened. It is not an infrequent complaint of parents that the child just breezed in and left quickly because he was "too busy" with group and peer activities. Nevertheless, the children rarely give up or avoid such visits completely. They wish to spend some time "with the parents."

Periodic reports about the progress of the group (and the individual children in it) are presented at parents' meeting by the metaplot as well as by the kindergarten teacher.

D. The "mixed" kindergarten

Child rearing and educational practices in the three federations of Kibbutzim are very similar. Differences, though not major ones, do exist, however, between some of the federations. One of these differences is particularly notable in the structure of the kindergarten.

Whereas one federation (Kibbutz Artzi) advocates the "peer" kindergarten (same age group), another one (Kibbutz M'uchad) advocates a "mixed" kindergarten with children of a wide age range; some as low as two years of age (depending on level of maturation) and all the way up to age seven.

The advocates of this multi-age kindergarten feel that it provides for a continuity in the kindergarten "culture." Not all children are moved *en masse* from the kindergarten into the second grade; only a few every year (those who have reached their seventh year and are of appropriate physical and intellectual maturity). Among the other advantages they list the function of the older children serving as an example to the younger ones, the opportunity for greater individuality of play and less uniformity than in the peer kindergarten, and a broader experience in interpersonal relationships. Under the mixed arrangement, the proponents claim, the child experiences fewer transfers from one house to another and resides continuously for about five important formative years in the same physical surroundings. On the other hand, the social environment changes as some children leave the group for the grade school and new ones enter every year. Established patterns of interpersonal relationships are not perpetuated throughout childhood, as may be the case in the peer-age kindergarten group.

THE CHILDREN'S SOCIETY—PRIMARY SCHOOL YEARS

A. *The school*

Following the years in kindergarten, the child is transferred to the elementary school, the pupils of which also constitute the younger "children's society." Since work, equivalent to that required in the conventional first grade, has already been done in the kindergarten, the school proper starts with grade 2 and ends with grade 6. Thus, the elementary school group ranges in age from seven to twelve years.

The second-graders move from the kindergarten into a new building, which is a combination of dormitory and classroom. The building usually accommodates 20 to 25 youngsters. Three or four youngsters sleep in each bedroom. The classroom is usually quite large and serves a variety of purposes in addition to instruction. It is often used for recreation, as a general meeting place for the group, and as a party room. Similar buildings are available for the other four grades in the elementary school system. In the more prosperous, well-established and well-planned Kibbutzim, this group of buildings are in a somewhat separate cluster. Adjacent to them are outdoor sports facilities, a small farm and gardens worked by the children themselves under the guidance of older children and adults.

Each grade that enters the school acquires a new metapelet and a teacher-counselor. Both stay with the group through the elementary school period, until age 12 when the children enter the Mosad or institute, which is equivalent to a combination of junior and senior high school in the United States.

The role of the metapelet from now on becomes less significant in the life of the youngster. She takes care of the physical needs, cleanliness, food, and order in the dormitory. In addition, her function tends to become that of a "housemother" in a dormitory or fraternity. On the other hand, the teacher, who is often a man, becomes a dominant figure of influence in the life of the children. His responsibilities go far beyond subject-matter instruction. He is teacher, counselor, work supervisor and the conscience of the group, all wrapped up in one. He is the one who is responsible for the morale of the group and for the development of its social consciousness; for setting up the complex organizational network within it, and for making it an integral part of the "children's society" (which will be discussed later, under C).

In the elementary school the child spends four to six hours daily (six days a week) on his studies. The first two grades (3 and 4) spend only four hours; grades 4 and 5, five hours; in grade 6 this is increased to full six hours of study a day. Most of the classes are generally conducted in the hours before noon.

One of the major tenets in Kibbutz ideology and in its philosophy of collective education is the inseparability of what may be termed "education" (studies) and "upbringing" (personality development). Both aspects are seen as a unitary process in the Kibbutz educational system. This philosophy determines the approach to the educational process, especially in the primary school setup.

In the first place, the group or the grade is set up as a cooperative rather than a competitive unit. The same level of achievement is not required of everybody. There is full recognition of individual differences in talents and abilities of the children despite the complete equality of opportunity in the egalitarian society of the Kibbutz. Every child is encouraged to follow his interests and do the best he can in contributing to the group effort. Consonant with this approach there is, of course, no grading system and "promotion" is assured for everybody. This arrangement demands a tremendous amount of devotion and individual work on the part of the teacher. His duties are far from over at the end of the more formal instructional period.

Secondly, the conventional division of the educational content into formal subject-matter or discrete "subjects" is rejected as artificial. Instead, the educational process in the primary grades is based on the "project" or "topic" method. Kibbutz educators feel that the studies should be directly related to life itself and to the manner in which the child perceives the world about him. Consequently, they feel that they should deal with whole "chunks" of life which cut across a number of conventional subjects. "Topics" are covered from many angles in periods from two to six weeks, depending on their importance. Some of the topics are: the forest, wheat and bread, the highway, our Kibbutz, our forefathers, our foods, the Kingdom in ancient Israel. In this manner a great many historical, biological and other scientific and literary materials are treated in their organic connection with the everyday reality of the child. The educators feel that the conventional subject division necessitates too many shifts daily from one area to another and impedes the concentrated attention of the child. The topic system also facilitates consideration of individual differences between the pupils and individual work as part of a larger collective plan—the project—on which everyone in the group is collaborating.

Finally, this system does not result in a *laissez faire* or a sloppy attitude with respect to school work. The pupils are inculcated with the idea that studies are not a voluntary matter just because there are no tests and no grades, but an important and significant social obligation which no member of the group (and of the children's society) can be permitted to abrogate or sabotage. This obligation combined with the project method (as a replacement for "subject matter") are responsible for the high level of motivation and interest frequently shown by the children in school work. To be sure, the pressure of the group (public opinion) and the threat of disapproval of adults (teacher and parents) are important factors in maintaining the motivational level of the child. Without the approval of the adults and, especially, of the peer group, the child loses self-esteem; he almost feels "annihilated." Kibbutz education quite consciously builds upon the authority of the teacher and upon the social authority of the peer group.

At the end of a study unit or a project, the group arranges a party; it is called a "summary" or "resume" party. At such a party each child has an opportunity to demonstrate what he has learned about the particular topic. Here again, individual achievement is not emphasized; the children participate in a group demonstration, such as a play, a mock trial, an exhibit, or a combination of all of these. It is the achievement of the group that is extolled rather than any individual virtuosity. At such parties the parents are often present, upon invitation. The child ordinarily insists that they come; and they do. It is through them that the child gets *his* personal recognition in contradistinction to the group recognition. *His* personal achievement is recognized and praised by the parents. This recognition of their individual and personal worth is very important to most of the children, especially in the primary grades.

B. The group

From early infancy onward, the Kibbutz child lives in a group. At first he is in the company of several other infants in the same room; this is not a "group" in the full meaning of the word. "Groupiness" or cohesiveness between several young infants cannot be expected. Attachments, however, between infants are often formed very early in life. Any metapelet can relate episodes of some infant "falling in love" with the infant in the next crib. The infant may watch his friend practically during all his waking hours, babble at him, and become extremely upset and morose when his friend happens to be moved to another room. Such separations have been known to cause loss of appetite and a run-down physical condition which improved upon reunion of the "twins."

In the nursery or in the toddlers house the children are grouped by room and by the metapelet who is in charge of them. There are attempts to organize group activities of the three- and four-year olds approval. However, at this level, the mutual help and the respect for the rights of other members of the group are most important. and to evolve a group morale consisting of group censure and group

When the children are transferred to the kindergarten, there is a temporary loosening of the old ties. There is a new group formation, and the groups are somewhat larger. Often, the children who belonged to the same toddlers group may form a cohesive "group within a group." Attempts are usually made by the organizers of the kindergarten to avoid such divisiveness. During the three years in the kindergarten, the group concept and group responsibility are not yet fully developed. To be sure, there are cooperative activities of the entire kindergarten, but little self-government of a group and, what is even more important, little if any formal or official relationship with other groups of children. This changes considerably when the child enters the second grade in school.

The group that becomes the second grade ordinarily remains stable for the following ten to eleven years—until the children graduate from high school (Mosad) at age 18. The principle of closeness in age is adhered to. The spread in age is, on the average, about six months. The group is a "living unit" as well as an educational *grade*. The group resides in the same dormitory, has the same metapelet and teacher, takes care of its house with the help of the adults, and takes care of its garden.

Every group conducts a series of autonomous and "internal" activities. It organizes hikes and outings, attends the theatre and movies as a unit, and demonstrates via exhibitions and via a variety of "end of the year" events its achievements during the past year to parents and to the entire Kibbutz. Private parties as well as birthday parties, to which the parents and siblings of the child are invited, are also arranged by the group.

As a study unit, or school grade, it completes a certain number of topics during the year. Informal activities, such as the hikes, parties and exhibitions, are frequently interwoven and related to the classroom material.

With the guidance of the teacher, and as a result of continuous sharing and living together collectively, there develops a "group conscience." Any deviation of the individual from proper behavior and any neglect of duty, whether work or academic, comes immediately to the attention of the rest of the group. At meetings of the group, which sometimes may take place daily, under the guidance of the teacher and at times without him, the offender may be brought to task. The group demands discipline and responsibility of the individual. The very knowledge of accountability to the group becomes a strong deterrent to deviant behavior. The individual is loath to incur group disapproval; "public opinion" of the group becomes most important in the life of the primary school child.

C. The "children's society"

Although the Kibbutz sees considerable advantage in the like-age smaller group, it is cognizant of the advantages that might accrue from contacts of younger and older children. The "children's society" was created to fulfill this function. It is essentially a federation of the primary grades 2 to 6, including all the children between the ages of seven to twelve.

As mentioned earlier, socially as well as geographically, the children's society forms a semi-autonomous unit within the larger Kibbutz society. The entire organization is governed by a children's "secretariat," consisting of representatives of each group or grade, with the participation of one of the teachers. The activities of this larger society are numerous, involving the work and care of an independent "farm," sports, editing a paper, cultural activities, etc. These activities are directed by committees selected at the general meetings of the society, which take place periodically several times a month. Each committee also includes a teacher among its members. Nearly every week there is a general party of the entire children's society. On such occasions each of the groups, constituting the society, participates actively in preparing a portion of the program, which may consist of music, songs, readings, dances or plays.

This complex organization provides a multitude of opportunities for interaction between the younger and older children. The latter are frequently helpful in tutoring the younger children and in training them in sports; on many other occasions, they function as older siblings.

The children's "farm" deserves special notice. It belongs to the children. It is a sort of miniature farm introduced into the educational system in order to establish early work habits and to get the children acquainted with the agricultural life, for at that level they do not yet participate substantially in the adult agricultural and economic enterprise. To a degree, the farm compensates for the discontinuity of children's roles and those of the adult world. The farm includes chickens, goats, rabbits and pigeons as well as small areas for planting and for grazing. In the work the children are guided and supervised by the teachers and, sometimes, by other adult Kibbutz members. Care is taken to rotate the children in their farm work. The younger ones are rotated fairly frequently—every week to a new activity. The older ones may spend one or two months on some particular job. The rotation is designed to maintain the interest of the child as well as offer him a greater variety of experiences in the different branches of the miniature economy.

In their house or dormitory the children are expected to do most of the chores that are involved in keeping the house in order. They sweep, clean, make their own beds, etc.

The total amount of house and farm work expected increases with age—from about half an hour daily for the younger children to about one and a half hours a day for the older ones.

The "Teens" in the Kibbutz—the Mosad

Ages 12 to 18 are represented by still another social organization within the Kibbutz, the older children's society—the society of adolescents. The organization has many features similar to those of the children's society, but some differences in structure and content do exist.

A. School—the Mosad

The last six grades constitute the Mosad (literally—institute). At approximately age 12 the children "graduate" from the 6th grade and from the children's society. The group as a whole is transferred to the final educational stage represented by the Mosad.

Some of the larger Kibbutzim maintain their own Mosad. Some of the Kibbutzim that do not have enough children in that age group or cannot afford their own institute band together with two or three others and establish a regional Mosad which serves the several settlements.

Physically and geographically the Mosad is more definitely a separate entity; it is usually built apart from the Kibbutz. In case of a regional Mosad, it may be built halfway between two Kibbutzim. Aside from the individual, grade-dormitory-classroom buildings, similar to those in the primary grades, there is a central dining room for pupils and teachers, similar to the ones available for the regular Kibbutz members. As in the Kibbutz, the Mosad dining room is the cultural and social center of the adolescent society. It serves as a meeting place for the entire Mosad. There parties are held, holidays are celebrated, and gatherings of a less formal nature take place. A library and reading room, a teachers' room, a music room, and physics, chemistry and biology laboratories are some of the other public buildings in the Mosad. Since the Mosad also has its own farm, there are farm buildings and shacks for tools and machinery.

In the average Mosad, there are around 200 pupils and a staff of about 20 or more teachers, counselors and metaplot. The grade size is the same or slightly larger than on the primary level. The curricular structure, however, changes markedly in the Mosad. The "project" method is no longer considered feasible at this level, and a conventional schedule of "split-up" subject matter takes its place. Two parallel curricula are offered—the "humanistic" and "realistic." The former encompasses such subjects as literature, sociology, history, economics; the latter is based on the sciences—physics, chem-

27

istry and biology. Both curricula offer instruction in Arabic and English, mathematics, drawing, music, physical education and shop.

B. Regrouping—the "adolescent society"

In most of the larger Kibbutzim whole groups of pupils transfer from the primary grades to the Mosad when they reach the right age. Often, however, there are changes in the membership of the groups. One important source of change is the regional Mosad where graduates from two or more primary schools enter and form new groups consisting of like-age youngsters from two or more Kibbutzim. Another source of change is the "outside" pupil. Beginning with the primary grades, but especially in the Mosad, children from the city or from a noncollective village are sometimes admitted, often for the remainder of their educational career. (It is not rare for these children to relinquish their outside ties and decide, upon graduation from the Mosad, to become members of a Kibbutz.) The Kibbutz school system is thus utilized by the outsiders as a "boarding school." Often they introduce discordant notes into the homogeneous Kibbutz-reared group. Though they are frequently met with hostility, especially by the younger members of the groups, adjustment and assimilation follow. These work both ways in that the newcomers introduce new values and customs into the group that absorbs them.

The outsiders are often blamed by the metaplot and others responsible for the Kibbutz children for introducing standards of morality different from those of Kibbutz children. We shall refer to this more specifically in a later discussion concerning the boy-girl relationships in the Kibbutz.

The adolescent society of the Mosad is organized pretty much along the lines of the children's society of the primary grades. Here, too, we have a federation of smaller groups—the educational, social and living units of the adolescents, corresponding to the academic grade levels. The same type of democratic organization of the group under the tutelage of the adult teacher-guide also prevails in the Mosad. The functions of the teacher and metapelet, however, are not quite so prominent in the guidance of the Mosad group as in the younger group. The adults function more in an advisory capacity, whereas the group with its committees and democratic institutions becomes dominant. This is especially so in the last two years of the Mosad, when the children are 17 and 18 years old.

An important supplement to the educational curriculum and social program of the adolescent society is the network of "circles." These are informal, voluntary groups formed by the youngsters. One evening a week is usually devoted to meetings of the different circles which are concerned with literature, arts and crafts, dramatics, music, agriculture, etc. The circles give children with special interests the opportunity to work and develop special knowledge in the subject areas of their choice. The circles are led and instructed by teachers and, sometimes, by other Kibbutz members who have achieved some expertness in that particular field of endeavor.

Music is particularly emphasized in the adolescent society. Every Mosad has its own choir or glee club, a small band or another type of orchestral organization. Youngsters who show aptitude for some particular instrument are given the opportunity for further training. Often such training is obtained through instruction with private teachers outside the Kibbutz.

Sports are by no means neglected. There is a good deal of competition between the several groups in the Mosad in such sports as basketball and volleyball; the competition extends to the inter-mosad level as well. It is a popular activity, and a good deal of the "free time" available in the life of the Kibbutz adolescent, male and female, is spent in training in their favorite sport. It is not part of the regular school curriculum but is encompassed within the evening and weekend activities of the circles.

The adolescents, like the younger children's society, maintain their own farm. This establishment is on a somewhat larger scale, more diversified, and requiring a good deal of work and skill of the youngsters. The farm may include sizable areas for vegetable gardens, feeds and other kinds of plants, as well as several hundred chickens, goats (for milking), a couple of horses, and even a small tractor as an aid in cultivation. The younger Mosad children work from one to two hours daily on their farm, whereas some of the

29

older ones may serve as instructors or be in charge of a particular branch of the venture. In many respects, a miniature Kibbutz economy, agriculturally and administratively, is represented by the farm and its management. The oldest children in the Mosad who are not engaged in the supervision of the younger ones become involved in the regular adult Kibbutz economic enterprise. They are expected, approximately from ages 16 to 18, to spend about three hours daily working in the various branches of the Kibbutz economy. At first they may spend about three months in each branch; later, six months or longer in one particular area of agricultural specialization. Thus, the youngsters serve a sort of limited apprenticeship which prepares them to become fairly versatile future members of the Kibbutz. Whereas the children's farms are designed as "educational or preparatory workshops, the work with the Kibbutz adults during the last two years is the "real thing."

The organization and administration of the work program in the Mosad is in the hands of a committee consisting of representatives of the different age groups. An older youngster (11th or 12th grader) is the responsible functionary in charge of the execution of the work program, advised and aided by one of the teachers or metaplot of the Mosad.

In addition to the agricultural work, shop work is required as a part of the school program. Three hours weekly are spent by the Mosad children in special shops; they are instructed by special teachers in wood work, book binding, metal work, needle work and the like.

Once a week the Mosad arranges a festive party or gathering devoted to some cultural pursuits of general interest. The meeting or party may be devoted to the celebration of a holiday (national or international), to current events, a famous personality, etc. The various cultural institutions of the Mosad, such as the glee club and the orchestra, are in action and on display on such occasions. Selected films are also shown once weekly.

Although the adolescent society is still a federation of smaller groups, the children tend to become involved more and more in the larger collectivity and its functions. Moreover, intimate relationships between fewer persons, in smaller groups, tend to develop and tend to detract somewhat from the importance of the like-age school grade group. Besides, as we pointed out, the homogeneity of the groups may also be disturbed by changes in their composition.

The youth movement

The youth movement in Israel is a highly visible phenomenon. There are a number of youth movements sponsored by different political and ideological interests. They serve an important educational function for the youth in the city as well as in the country.

Kibbutz children's societies, especially those of the *Kibbutz Artzi* federation, are also branches of a larger national youth movement. A major characteristic of such movements is that the leadership, with the exception of the highest echelons, is in the hands of the youths themselves. The leader is usually only several years older than the members of his group. He is usually a responsible adolescent who is cognizant of the values of adult society and, yet, is sufficiently close psychologically to the members of the group in his charge. This leader, "Madrich" (instructor) emerges from the older grades of the Mosad, after some years experience as a member of a group himself.

The youth movement functions in a parallel fashion to the Mosad activities. There is usually a nearly complete overlap between the membership in the children's and adolescent societies and that of the youth movement. The latter, however, being a branch of a national movement, brings the children together on different occasions, from a variety of localities. On special occasions, such as hikes, celebrations, overnight camping trips, the Kibbutz children meet their city cousins who are members of the same movement. They participate in the same ceremonials, compete in scouting activities, and help to form a "style of life" and modes of behavior unique to the movement. It is in this youth movement that the independence of the children reaches the high point.

A question may be raised as to the special value of the youth movement in the Kibbutz. The Kibbutz child already possesses a great deal of autonomy via the very structure of the educational system and his life in a society of peers. The values that accrue to the child raised in the conventional family or to the child that lives "anonymously" in the large city are probably greater.

At any rate, the youth movement embroils the Kibbutz child in still another activity which moves him beyond the physical and psychological boundaries of his own settlement. This activity is in addition to the numerous other interests which claim his daily attention. It is not surprising that the Kibbutz adolescent spends less and less time in the family circle. Usually affectional ties to the family are being maintained and continued, but not in a very demonstrative fashion.

KIBBUTZ COEDUCATION

Consonant with the general ideological orientation of the Kibbutz, complete equality of the sexes is a cherished ideal. This ideal is reflected in the equal and non-differential treatment of boys and girls in the educational system—in "collective education." In the Kibbutz set-up, coeducation reaches the ultimate. It is not confined to school activities, i.e., boys and girls having classes together; both sexes actually *live* together, from infancy to maturity.

After leaving the toddlers' house, the boys and girls continue to share sleeping quarters until they graduate from the Mosad at age 18. There is no separation between the sexes in the dormitories or even in the shower room. Boys and girls shower together—theoretically, until adulthood. In practice, however, the pubescent girls, especially those who have developed fairly obvious secondary sexual characteristics, maneuver to take their showers when the boys are not around and develop a good deal of modesty with respect to their body.

Leaders in Kibbutz child rearing or in collective education have always insisted upon this principle of what we might call absolute coeducation. They feel that it creates a healthy relationship between the sexes; removes the mystery from sexual differences and from the appearance of the body of the opposite sex; and, in general, takes care of "sex education" in an informal and, presumably, effective manner.

Many of the parents of the children, Kibbutz members, have some doubts about the desirability of this system. Perhaps their own taboos and inhibitions come to play in pronouncing judgment. At any rate, it is probably these influences and influences from the "outside" that affect the adolescents, especially the girls, and create a "modesty problem" in the dormitories of the Mosad.

The outside influences come from two sources. First, the occasional visits of the Kibbutz child to the city, in the homes of relatives and friends, communicate to him the more conventional values with respect to body exposure. Second, the introduction of outside pupils into the school and into the Mosad inevitably entails the introduction of certain taboos and conventional attitudes which infiltrate the larger group. The educators see the outside as the source of modesty during adolescence; many parents with ambivalent attitudes about the system see the source in "human nature"—in natural modesty coming forth.

Thus, although the adolescent boys and girls may share sleeping rooms and shower facilities, most of the time they manage to avoid self exposure. Going to bed at different times, undressing in the dark, showering at different times are some of the techniques that have developed in the service of modesty and sexual segregation.

It may well be that the modesty that develops is in the service of defense against the instinctual drives that are intensified during adolescence. Despite the "freedom" with respect to viewing the body of the opposite sex, Kibbutz taboos and prohibitions in regard to sex-play and sexual contacts are strict and unrelenting. These taboos apply primarily to members of the peer-group, with whom the contact is continuous for many years. The taboos are not unlike the brother-sister taboos in the conventional family. It is probably due to this fact that there are few marriages between members of the same group in the Kibbutz. Such "incestuous" relationships are avoided by marrying outside the group, often into another Kibbutz or by importation of a spouse from the city.

The official attitude of the Kibbutz movement as well as that of the youth movement toward premarital intercourse or sex play is negative. "Friendships" with the opposite sex are encouraged;

33

sexuality without love is discouraged and considered base and degrading. The attitude is that the capacity to experience "true love," of which sexuality is only a part, is reached upon maturity and not before then. If maturity is reached and true love is achieved, then marriage is the natural consequence.

TRAINING AND EDUCATION BEYOND THE SECONDARY SCHOOL LEVEL

Kibbutz society is not content to go down in history as a "noble experiment" that was not viable. The Kibbutz movement is convinced of the advantages of its form of life and of the supreme value in its perpetuation. It wishes to place its trust in the new generation that knew no other form of life than the Kibbutz; it expects it to have none of the conflicts and ambivalences that the generation of "transition," the founders, experienced, who consciously relinquished one form of life to embrace another. The new generation is expected to adhere naturally to the form of life into which it was born.

The Kibbutz society endeavors to prepare its children for life *in the Kibbutz*. Thus, psychologically, physically, educationally and occupationally the aims of child rearing and education converge. Further educational plans and occupational choice are geared to the needs of the Kibbutz rather than to upward mobility in the outside competitive society. Professionalism and advanced specialization at the university level in areas not relevant to the Kibbutz economy or to the advancement of its teaching and cultural program are definitely discouraged.

Furthermore, the cost of higher education, and the loss of manpower to the Kibbutz, involved in sending away the Mosad graduates to the university, or other specialized institutes, are considerable deterrents.

Finally, there is the psychological aspect that many Kibbutz members would admit with some reluctance. Sending a youngster away for long periods of time into the outside world has its dangers. He may be weaned away from Kibbutz values and ideology and become so involved in the new society that it may claim him. At any rate, there is no wish to expose the Kibbutz child to outside temptations which may make his readjustment to the Kibbutz rather difficult.

Considering these reservations, what are the post-secondary-level training opportunties offered by the Kibbutzim? In the first place, the Kibbutz needs teachers at all levels and trained metaplot, especially for the infants. A teachers' seminary ("Seminar Hakibbutzim") is maintained by the Kibbutz movement, staffed by Kibbutz members and by outsiders. When the need arises in a Kibbutz, it may send as many of its young people as necessary for a two to three year teachers training course in the seminary. Some of the Mosad teachers may be sent to the University in Jerusalem for an extra year or two of advanced study in the physical sciences or languages. The decision as to who to send, and for how long, is usually made by the entire Kibbutz upon recommendation of an appropriate personnel committee.

Some Kibbutz members who have indicated an interest and aptitude may be sent away for varying periods of time to nurses' training courses, special agricultural and engineering institutes, etc., providing the Kibbutz sees the need for such advanced instruction.

Special talent is recognized, particularly in the arts. Such talented persons may be given the opportunity for further study through private instruction from experts (as in music) or in advanced schools. Only exceptional talent is nurtured in this manner.

Generally, however, the Kibbutz does not send out its young people (after they have served their stint in the Army), to colleges and universities. They continue in a variety of positions and jobs for which there is demand in the multi-faceted Kibbutz economy. To be sure, "education" continues on an informal level—in "circles" of study during the evenings, through reading, discussion and, occasionally, special workshops on specific topics. When one observes the "bustling" cultural activities of the younger generation in the Kibbutzim, it is difficult to share Koestler's (1946) nostalgia for the intellectualism of their fathers. Although the Kibbutz-reared young people may not be eggheads, they are far from representing a generation of "country bumpkins."

35

The problem of advanced training and education is not completely settled in the Kibbutz movement. From the utilitarian point of view, the question of obtaining sufficient professional personnel, such as architects, engineers, veterinarians and physicians, is of considerable moment. Should such personnel be obtained and educated within the Kibbutzim, or should the movement become increasingly dependent upon trained outsiders? The arguments *pro* and *con* are numerous and need not be listed at this juncture.

Not all considerations are utilitarian. There seems to be a good deal of clamor for advanced education among the young. Many wish to broaden their horizon and increase their potential contribution to the community. They also wish to attain a feeling of self-realization through self-development and training to the extent permitted by their abilities and talents. That these young people may be the future leaders of the Kibbutz movement is perceived by the present leaders. But these are problems that may not be solved for some time to come.

SUMMARY AND RECAPITULATION

In describing in some detail the process of child rearing and education in the Kibbutz, we have attempted to include all factors relevant to personality development without evaluation or bias. To be sure, the idea of "relevance" may introduce a certain selectivity. The account, of course, could have been expanded, but additional descriptive detail would bear little or no relationship to the crucial issues which are to be dealt with in the subsequent chapters.

The summary that follows will deal with the topics that cut across the different age levels which have served as reference points in our description.

A. Significant figures—adults and children

The first and foremost issue that needs careful treatment is that of the early and continuous interpersonal relationships of the child. Here we are particularly concerned with those persons who are in a position to exert an important influence upon the growing youngster due to their specific roles in relation to him.

During the early formative years the adults are of particular significance as sources of affection, nurturence and security, and as agents of socialization and transmitters of the cultural values. We shall review the sequence of adults in the life of the child, with some attention to the temporal dimension.

The *mother* is in close and almost continuous contact with the infant during the earliest period of life—the first four months or so. During that period her relation to the infant does not differ from that of a mother in the nuclear family setting. The main exception is that the mother is usually unavailable to the infant during the night. Between the ages of four to nine months, the mother's contact with the child is reduced considerably for she returns to full-time work. Breast feeding may be confined to twice daily, and gradual transition to solids (not handled by the mother as a rule) takes place. Contacts, therefore, between mother and child are reduced to two periods, of one or one and a half hours each—morning and late afternoon or early evening when the mother may put the infant to bed for the night. Following the ninth month (and often two to three months later) the mother's contacts are further reduced —to a daily after-work visit with the child, usually in the parents' quarters; for longer periods on rest days. At such times the mother (and father) is entirely "at the service" of the child (or of the children in the case of the child who is not the oldest or who is not an only child). This pattern of contact continues throughout the life of the Kibbutz child. As he grows older, of course, the frequency and duration of such contacts are increasingly under his own control.

Contacts with the *father* during the first year of life are during brief visits in the infant house, usually after working hours. Subsequently, the visits follow the same pattern as with the mother.

The *metapelet,* of course, is a very significant figure. We should speak of her in the plural, metaplot, for the child has several during his lifetime. The first metapelet is the one of the first nine months of life. Approximately during the first half of this period, the metapelet merely supplements the care given the infant by his biological mother. She takes care of the infants between the feeding periods

37

when they are asleep a good deal of the time. From the fifth month on, the metapelet begins to come into focus as a "socializing" agent. She introduces the infants to solids and takes over many of the functions, in addition to feeding, which were hitherto within the domain of the mother. After this partial transition from mother to metapelet has taken place, still another switch occurs. The infants' metapelet relinquishes her duties when the infants are weaned (she starts another group of newborn infants) and passes on her functions to a "regular" or permanent metapelet who takes over for the next several years.

The permanent metapelet sees the children through the toddler period and often well into the kindergarten. She is the one who carries the burden of the most important socialization functions in early childhood. She teaches them self-feeding, bowel and bladder control, some rudiments of group living and mutual respect, and many other habits that are part of the civilizing process. The functions of the permanent metapelet are probably the most important from the point of view of personality formation of the children. They are more important than the functions any other metapelet will have.

When the child reaches kindergarten, or sometime thereafter, his group may acquire a new metapelet. From now on, however, the metapelet is shared by the larger, combined kindergarten group consisting of twelve to eighteen children. The focus begins to shift away from the metapelet. She continues with the physical care of the children, but the force of leadership and a good deal of authority are lodged in the person of the kindergarten teacher.

Subsequently, through the grades and in the Mosad, the youngsters may have a succession of metaplot who are included in the over-all educational planning but are involved largely in housekeeping and technical functions. Group leadership becomes the prerogative of the teacher-educator-counselor (all one person) when the children, at age seven, join the children's society, beginning with the second grade of school.

The *teacher* generally accompanies the same group of children for several years, through the sixth grade. Not only does he (or she) teach the subject matter (via projects), but he also serves as coun-selor, guide, and general adult authority. He is available to the children not only during the hours of instruction, but evenings and sometimes weekends as well. He settles disputes among the children in the group meetings and aids in the further socialization process. He is a representative of the Kibbutz, and imparts its morality and ideology to the youngsters during the latency period.

In the Mosad a new group leader-educator is appointed. He, too, is a teacher, usually of one or two subjects, for in the Mosad the project method is abandoned and the conventional division into subject matter is adopted. He may teach these subjects to his group as well as to other grade groups. However, as regards guidance, leadership and authority, his functions are confined to one group only. The adolescents view him as a representative of the adult world and come to terms with that world under his tutelage.

The *youth leader* is also an effective mediator between adolescence and adulthood. In age he is close to his group and probably understands its members better than does the adult. Yet, he is usually sufficiently mature to influence the adolescent in the direction of adult morality and ideology which he represents. He can identify with the adolescents' needs more easily and can serve as leader, companion, and "father confessor" with greater facility than the adult who may be a member of another generation.

In the life of the Kibbutz child there are figures that have *group* significance and those that have *individual* or *personal* significance. He often refers to the metapelet as "ours" (the group's); however, the parents are referred to as "mine." This distinction is created early and is maintained as additional adult figures enter the child's life.

Children who are members of the group in which the Kibbutz youngster grows up are also significant figures in his life. He shares with them most of his waking hours and sleeps in the same room or the same house with them. Later they are members of the same grade, work on the same projects, and are under the same watchful eye of the teacher. In many ways they are like siblings; probably more like twins, for the age differential characteristic of siblings in

39

the biological family is lacking. Often, close friendships between individuals and patterns of identification are observable.

B. The group factor

The group has something that goes beyond the individuals who comprise it. From the very beginning, collective education is geared to group life and group upbringing—preparatory for later sharing and living together in the collectivity or in the communal society which is the Kibbutz.

The Kibbutz child is born into and spends the rest of his childhood with the peer group. The group is viewed not as a mere collection of individuals, but as an entity in its own right. Around the third year of life, in the toddlers house, emphasis on group living commences. The sharing of food, toys and goodies, group activities, respect for the rights of others receive their rudimentary emphasis. As the child progresses through kindergarten and the grades, it is group rather than individual achievement that is stressed. As an individual he is judged by the group, on the basis of his effort and contribution to the group endeavor. In school, too, he contributes his share to the project which is a group activity. His failure to perform the functions placed upon him, be it performing at a party of the children's community or keeping his room clean, is viewed as a betrayal of the group. Judgment and reactions come swiftly, and group ostracism may be quickly felt. Group disapproval and ostracism is to be avoided at all costs. Group pressure and group opinion are powerful influences in keeping each child in line. On the other hand, group cohesiveness and solidarity give him a feeling of strength and security. As he grows up, he often may have difficulty in imagining himself alone, acting on his own entirely, without his peers watching over his shoulder.

C. Education and coeducation

Since each grade—in kindergarten, in primary school, in the Mosad—is also a group and a living unit, the physical arrangements are designed correspondingly. Each group has its own building—consisting of living quarters for all members of the group and a classroom-clubroom combination. Generally, these houses are well equipped. Children come first, and are given the best the Kibbutz can afford.

Child rearing and education are as completely coeducational as one can imagine. No distinction in functions, duties and obligation between the sexes is made. Segregation of the sexes is nonexistent. Boys and Girls live in the same quarters from infancy through the period of adolescence. The same bathing facilities are used. (However, around the beginning of puberty the girls manage to avoid the unsegregated showers.) Concomitant with this freedom there are, however, strong taboos with respect to sex play and premarital intercourse. These taboos are constantly supported by the adult leadership, the youth leaders, and the groups themselves.

D. Youth culture

Kibbutz children are reared exclusively in groups composed of their age peers. Their contacts with the biological parents are relatively limited. Other adults interact with Kibbutz children primarily in their capacity as cultivators of the children's societies or of what might be termed the youth culture.

The school-age children of the Kibbutz are divided into two "societies"—the children's society (primary school) and the adolescent society (Mosad). Each society is a federation of several smaller groups which correspond to the classroom grades. All of the activities of the children take place in *their* world, in their societies, but not in the adult's world or in his society. The main reference point of the child is the group of peers rather than the family consisting of adults and other children of different ages. There is an age range within the societies of the children, for each spans about five to six years of the child's life, but the same age prevails in the intimate smaller groups which make up the federated society.

Work and training for work is part of the childhood experience, but the Kibbutz child does not, until the later teens, become involved in the work world of the adult. Almost until he becomes an adult himself, he works on the children's farms for relatively short periods of time every day. These are sort of "make believe" farms,

41

for nobody depends upon their income and productivity. Still they represent a "dress rehearsal" for adult living. There is no integration with the workaday world of adult society—its worries, cares, anxieties, and aspirations. The children remain distant from this world and are shielded against it through the network of childhood institutions—through the youth culture.

There may be some merit to the ideas of Kibbutz educators that training in age-homogeneous groups is the best way to perpetuate Kibbutz life. The schema, however, does not provide for role-continuity between child and adult.

3.

Problems Posed
by Collective Education

A description of child rearing practices and education in the Kibbutz may be of interest in itself. We have presented the material here because the Kibbutz setting serves as a "laboratory" for testing many generalizations and hypotheses concerning child rearing and the relationship of early childhood experience to later personality development. Collective education affords us the opportunity to examine some of our notions that stem primarily from data obtained from the nuclear family of Western society. Many of our principles and conclusions about child rearing are probably culture bound, yet their universal applicability is almost invariably implied. In this chapter we shall see what some of the principles and ideas, facts and generalizations are that may be questioned in the light of the Kibbutz experience. In subsequent chapters we will attempt to deal systematically with a number of the crucial issues we are about to stir up.

CLINICAL OBSERVATIONS

A description of child rearing in the Kibbutz, combined with some clinical observations regarding the mental health of Kibbutz children, presented at a conference in 1953, stimulated a great many questions among the participants (Caplan, 1954). Basically, the material was the same as published earlier by Irvine (1952). In addition to the description of collective education, Caplan presented some "clinical impressions" based on his own observations and on those of his colleagues. Essentially, he noted certain changes in the mental health picture and emotional life of Kibbutz children in the course of their development. Such observations, of course, were not longitudinal, but were made of Kibbutz children at different age levels. The implicit assumption (not unreasonable) is that these cross-sectional observations and impressions may be placed in a sequence and, thus, portray the developmental course of the Kibbutz child.

The findings were that "children below the age from about five to seven, and particularly the toddlers, manifest symptoms which, in our Western culture, we would feel to be signs of emotional disturbance. There is a tremendous amount of thumbsucking, temper tantrums, and general lack of control over aggression—much more so than among children raised in families. "Enuresis is endemic" (Caplan, p. 98). However, somehow or other, a change occurs after age six or seven. The "incidence of signs of disturbance falls. . . . By the time they reach the age of about ten or eleven, the signs of emotional disturbance . . . appear only about as frequently as they do . . . in our culture." Caplan goes on to note that "They have a much smoother adolescence than our children, and as young adults they are remarkably non-neurotic."

Thus, it can be stated that Kibbutz children, despite a "bad start" during the first few years of life, show a capacity to overcome this handicap and lead an emotionally normal life. In the first few years they "look as though they are suffering from maternal deprivation." The latter observation is, of course, loaded with certain assumptions and theoretical preconceptions. On the other hand, the observation that disturbed emotional life in early childhood did not leave its marks upon, nor did it visibly affect, the stability of the adolescents and adults is a remarkable one. It is unusual for it goes against some of our basic understanding, against principles and psychodynamics of personality development. The participants of the 1953 conference were readily willing to accept the observations of the earlier years of Kibbutz child development, but had difficulty in accepting the subsequent "improvement" and change at its face value. The impressions concerning the early years "fitted" into the theoretical framework; the observations about the preadolescent to the adult years did not.

Many of the questions raised by the participants "have been directed," as Fremont-Smith pointed out, "to finding the weak spot in the system." Some of these questions may be condensed and summarized as follows:

a. To what extent is there a sort of "homogenization" of children in the Kibbutz, e.g., a reduction of individual differences due to the uniformity in the upbringing and child rearing practices?
b. Can the post-adolescent Kibbutz product be really accepted as an emotionally mature individual?
c. Did not the adolescents and young adults (who were observed) differ as young children from the ones included in the report?

Three alternatives come to mind when one tries to deal with the dilemma that emanates from the report. In the first place, perhaps child rearing in the Kibbutz cannot be subsumed under the rubric of "maternal deprivation." Second, the symptoms such as enuresis, thumbsucking, etc., judged as indicating emotional disturbance in our culture, do not have the same meaning in other cultural settings. Third, perhaps human beings have greater capacity for flexibility than we give them credit for. Even emotionally disturbed young children may be exposed, subsequent to the pre-school years, to certain "corrective" experiences that may effect reintegration and facilitate ego growth and development.

Maternal Deprivation

Explicitness and specificity are not major characteristics of the concept "maternal deprivation." It is a global clinical concept which covers a large variety of phenomena and deals with numerous situations in which mothering is not performed in the manner typical in the nuclear family of Western Society. Yarrow (1961) suggests a

45

fourfold classification of settings that represent "deviations" in maternal care.

Institutionalization—a situation where the child is cared for by different adults, none of whom is a real mother surrogate. The relationship is impersonal and noncontinuous.

Separation from a mother figure (biological mother or substitute) with whom a close and warm relationship has been established in the family setting.

Table 3-1 The family, institution and Kibbutz as structural models for adult-child interaction*

Factor	Family	Institution	Kibbutz
1. Number of children per adult	Low	High	Medium
2. Continuity of adult-child interaction	High	Low	Variable
3. Specificity of adult-child emotional response	High	Low	Medium
4. Warmth and intensity of adult emotional response	High	Low	High
5. Adult approval and reward	High	Low	High
6. Gratification of tensions	Rapid, magical, achieved effortlessly	Unpredictable	Variable — depending on time of day
	Influenced quickly by child's own demands	Determined by group routine	Variable — depending on time of day
7. Richness of environmental stimulation	High	Low	High
8. Stereotypy in environmental stimulation	Low	High	Variable

*Adapted from W. Goldfarb — Emotional and intellectual consequences of psychological deprivation. In Hoch & Zubin, (Eds.) *Psychopathology of childhood,* Grune & Stratton: 1955

46

Multiple mothering—situations which are for the most part not impersonal but in which two or more persons may perform the mothering functions, i.e., discontinuity in the maternal figure.

Distortion in mothering—a condition which has been studied for the most part in the family setting, representing such phenomena as rejection, over-protection, and inconsistency in attitude on the part of the mother.

Most of the studies concerning maternal deprivation are based on the first two types of situation—institutionalization and separation. The former in particular is relevant to our analysis of the experiences of Kibbutz children, for many have likened the Kibbutz child rearing process to that prevalent in institutions, summarized in Bowlby's (1951) well known review monograph. Before we discuss the effects of maternal deprivation *à la* institutions, it may be well to ask the question: "To what extent is institutional child rearing really comparable to the Kibbutz child rearing program?

In a summary article on "Emotional and intellectual consequences of psychologic deprivation in infancy," Goldfarb (1955) presents a table in which he compares the institution with the typical family on a number of factors which he considers relevant to deprivation. It may be noted that he shifts his emphasis from the relatively narrow concept of maternal deprivation to the broader one of *psychologic* deprivation. We are including an additional column on the Kibbutz for comparative purposes (Table 3-1).

1. Number of children per adult

The differences between the ordinary family and the institution with respect to this variable are quite obvious. The ratio of children to adults is much greater in institutions, where an adult has a fairly large number of children under his care. Not so in the family, with the possible exception of extremely large families, where the number of children per adult is small; usually about one or two during the period of infancy. In the Kibbutz the ratio is somewhere in between these two extremes, especially during the latter part of the first year of life and onward. The metapelet has four to six children to care for, with no male adults regularly available (as in the ordinary family). The child-adult ratio in the family is smaller and in the institution, usually, larger than in the Kibbutz.

2. Continuity of adult-child interaction

With respect to this allegedly crucial dimension (Bowlby, 1951), the comparison is not so simple or clear-cut. To be sure, in the family continuity is high, whereas in institutions it is low because of the frequent changes in the adults, in the personnel, who have charge of a particular child. However, the situation in the Kibbutz poses a special question. Does "continuity" refer to continuous contact between the adult and child during all hours of the day, or are daily contacts during certain times of the day with the same adult(s) sufficient to provide a state of continuity? Is the situation in Kibbutz child rearing one of "intermittent" mothering (Rabin, 1958) or is it more adequately described as one of "concomitant" mothering? If we view the metapelet only, we may note discontinuity, for a new one appears for the child toward the end of his first year of life. On the other hand, if we consider the biological mother, there *is* continuity, from day to day, for many years. Thus, the Kibbutz combines, with respect to continuity, some aspects of the family and the institution; it is both high and low on this dimension. This specific situation should lead us to a more refined conceptualization and definition of the term continuity as it applies to early parent-child relationships.

3. Specificity of adult-child emotional response

Continuity in interaction creates the conditions for the specificity of emotional response. Hence, specificity is high in the family and low in the institution. In the Kibbutz we, again, encounter a dual, or parallel, state of affairs. With respect to the relationship to the parents, there is a high degree of specificity of emotional response. The biological parents, although concerned about all the children in the Kibbutz, are particularly involved with and affectionate toward their own. The children, on their part, speak of "*my* mother" but of "*our* metapelet." The metapelet is the one who provides a more objective attitude and nonspecific, nonpreferential

48

emotional response to the children in her group. In practice she is not always "objective" and has her favorites in the group. However, as a rule, her nonspecific response exists simultaneously with the definitely specific one of the child's mother and father. Here too a simple "high" or "low" would not provide a complete evaluation of the state of affairs in the Kibbutz.

4. Warmth and intensity of adult emotional response

Variation from the previous factor to this one is small. Ordinarily the emotional response of the adult in the family is warm and intense; in the institution, impersonal attitudes predominate, and warmth and emotional intensity of a positive nature are lacking. If anything, the Kibbutz child enjoys an extremely affectionate attitude during his visits with his parents. The needs of some of the parents, especially the mothers, in relation to the children become expressed in a very intense and affectionate form and in a concentrated fashion during the visiting hours. The metapelet is also a warm figure, but her emotional response, of necessity and by design, is less intense. Thus, for the Kibbutz this variable may be rated as high.

5. Adult approval and reward

Both, in the family and in the Kibbutz, adult approval and reward are high as compared with conditions at the institution. The Kibbutz parents are a very potent source of gratification and reward. Since they are not involved very much in the socialization process, the connection between their rewards and undesirable behavior is not an important one in the case of the Kibbutz child. For similar reasons (i.e., they do not witness much of the child's antisocial behavior), their approval is high. The approval and reward of the metapelet is linked with the socialization process. Approval, encouragement and rewards rank high among the socializing techniques. However, as in the ordinary family, disapproval by the metapelet (and later, by the group), and punishment are also part of the "civilizing" procedure employed.

49

6. Gratification of tensions

This is one of the areas in which the nursery or the children's house in the Kibbutz differs markedly from the family and the individual home. In the family, tensions or needs are gratified rapidly, magically, without much effort on the part of the infant and without the experience of excessive frustration. In the Kibbutz, the situation is not so ideal. Although the mother is available to the infant in the Kibbutz at frequent intervals during the first weeks of life, her presence in the nursery is not continuous. The metapelet, who has several children to care for, is not in a position to effect immediate gratification and relief of tension. To some extent the situation is unpredictable—similar to that existing in the institution—particularly after the first two months or so when the mother becomes available at less frequent intervals. The special circumstances of the Kibbutz infant at night increase this unpredictability, for at that time neither mother nor metapelet is available, and the response of the night watchwoman is neither rapid nor magical.

In addition to the anticipation of the child's demands in the family setting, there is also an immediate response of the environment to the child's demands resulting in a gratification of needs and reduction of tensions. The child influences the quick response of the family. In the institution, the determining factor in gratification of needs is group routine rather than individual demands. In this respect, the institution is perhaps closer to the Kibbutz than is the conventional family. So that the metapelet may function efficiently, some kind of routine or program has to be developed for the group of children in her care. Eating, sleeping, bathing, etc., are according to a schedule; also, every child is taken "in turn" to be fed, bathed, etc., while the others must wait. Although the group is the primary determinant, attempts at flexibility are being made on the part of the metaplot.

7. Richness of environmental stimulation

Environmental stimulation may be roughly divided in two types, the interpersonal and the physical environment.

In the family, Goldfarb (1955) feels, the mother-child inter-action "offers *constant stimulation.*" The physical handling of the child by his mother, being talked to and sung to, and her reacting to the child's efforts at "active mastery" are important sources of stimulation to the child. Such experiences are not common in the life of the institutional child; the stimulation is impoverished. In the Kibbutz, with the low adult-child ratio during most of the day, such intensive stimulation is not available; a good deal is concentrated in the visiting hours with the biological parents. Then, stimulation is at a maximum. Consequently, we cannot say that with respect to richness of environmental stimulation our rating would be either "high" or "low"; it is a combination of the two.

With respect to the physical environment, the Kibbutz situation is probably similar to the family situation in which the environment is "filled with numberless objects—toys, animals, people, household implements." From our description of the infants' and toddlers' houses and their physical arrangements, one could readily see that awareness of need for physical stimulation underlies the planning. The toys, yard, trips, as well as the contacts with additional toys in the parents' quarters, are all indications of the richness of the physical environment. There certainly is no deprivation with respect to sensory stimulation from the enviroment. The situation in the Kibbutz, in this respect, is not at all comparable to that of the institution.

8. *Stereotypy in environmental stimulation*

If "stereotypy" means sameness and lack of variability in the environmental stimulation, then our rating of the Kibbutz child rearing process would be placed somewhere between family (low) and institution (high).

The Kibbutz child rather early in life is subjected to some kind of group routine and regulation. "Group requirements and program needs dominate the individual child's own wishes and inclinations." (Goldfarb, 1955). However, he does encounter many environmental reactions (and stimulation) which may be resulting from his own "assertive expression" and idiosyncratic behavior. This picture would be incomplete if the interaction in the family circle at the parents' quarters or in their company outside these quarters is not taken into consideration. There, anything but routine and stereotypy are characteristic. Thus, the Kibbutz child, as in many other respects, seems to shuttle back and forth between two types of environments and interpersonal relationships which are entirely different from each other; from high child-adult ratio to low child-adult ratio (with parents), from group routine and domination to the indulgent parents with whom he is "king," from the relatively impersonal, "efficient" metapelet to the highly personal, emotionally involved parents. This shuttling back and forth certainly reduces stereotypy markedly.

Using Goldfarb's model, for a comparison of adult-child interaction in the family and in the institution, we come to the conclusion that the interaction of the Kibbutz child is identical with neither of these institutions and similar to both of them in some respects.

One of the major characteristics of the early experience of the Kibbutz infant and child is that of *alternation* or fluctuation in the nature of his interaction with adults. This fluctuation occurs daily in the life of the infant and toddler. During a certain period, or periods (first two months), of the day the experience of the Kibbutz infant resembles that of the family child; it is probably more intense in terms of warmth, affection, specificity in emotional response and approval. However, during most of the day and all of the night, the interaction is less intense, less warm and not as specific in emotional response. It may be speculated that in the early life of the infant this shifting back and forth and the changing expectancies may be frustrating and place a considerable burden upon his frail adaptive mechanisms. Such may be the experience of the infant until he establishes a certain *rhythm* and a capacity for adjusting his needs and anticipations to that temporal rhythm.

Because there is a relatively large child-adult ratio in the nursery, reduction of tensions is not as instantaneous and magical as in the family; it is more unpredictable. Hence, following dynamic theory, certain feelings of insecurity, due to the uncertainty of the environmental response, must be part of the picture. Frustration of

52

the feeling of omnipotence must take place early in the experience of the Kibbutz child.

All this, of course, is due to the program of "double mothering" which characterizes Kibbutz child rearing. With respect to environmental stimulation, the situation does not differ markedly from the favorable conditions in the family.

There is a richness both in the physical and in the human environment. Due to group living, the environment of the Kibbutz infant may be somewhat more stereotyped.

It is important to stress that the polarities set up were to some extent artificial: the family being all "good" and the institution, all "bad." The family is portrayed as the warm, nurturent, stimulating and constant environment, whereas the institution is the opposite. The actual state of affairs does not really follow or justify such a dichotomy. Some family environments are relatively cold and impersonal, while some institutions provide warmth and even continuity in adult-child relationships.

We have pointed out earlier that "psychologic deprivation" discussed in this section is a broader concept than maternal deprivation which may be an important component of it. Bowlby (1951), however, focused entirely on "maternal" deprivation as a menace to mental health. Moreover, his maternal deprivation is fundamentally based on the continuity hypothesis. At the outset of his monograph, he states that ". . . what is believed to be essential for mental health is that the infant and young child should experience a warm, intimate and continuous relationship with his mother (or permanent mother-substitute) in which both find satisfaction and enjoyment."

With respect to the Kibbutz, Bowlby (1951) gathers from his informants that there is "no complete abandonment of parent-child relations. Though the amount of time parents spend with their children is far less than in most other Western communities, the reports make clear that the parents are extremely important people in the children's eyes, and the children, in the parents'." Hence, Bowlby also sees partial deprivation, but sees continuity and positive relationships as well. Yet he comments that "it is by no means certain that the children do not suffer from this regime." He does, however, accept the observations regarding the relatively good adjustment of Kibbutz children later in life, but holds "that there is no evidence here which can be held to invalidate the hypothesis." Finally, despite these assertions and continued faith in his hypotheses, Bowlby still feels that "the conditions (in the Kibbutz) provide, of course, unusually rich opportunities for research in child development, and it is hoped these will not be missed." We propose to take up some of the challenge.

Since we have alluded in several places to the unhealthy effects of maternal deprivation, we shall now turn more specifically to these consequences. We shall also concern ourselves with the specific observations and indices of poor mental health in the Kibbutz setting.

ON THE CONSEQUENCES OF DEPRIVATION

After a fairly comprehensive survey of a great many reports on maternal deprivation, broadly defined, Bowlby (1951) admits that "there are still far too few systematic studies and statistical comparisons in which proper control groups have been used." Despite the admitted scientific inadequacy of many of the studies cited, he feels that the preponderance of the evidence points in the direction of the deleterious effects of maternal deprivation on later personality development. Under the term "maternal deprivation" he lumps together institutionalization during the first three years of life during which no opportunity to form an attachment to a mother figure is available; seperation from the mother for several months during these early years of life; and changes in the mother figure during the same years. These experiences "can each produce the affectionless and psychopathic character."

Some of the most systematic studies, including controls, which are discussed in detail by Bowlby are those of Goldfarb (1943a, 1943b, 1944, 1944, 1947). The data were obtained from follow-up studies of 15 institutionalized children subsequently placed in foster homes compared with 15 children who were placed in foster homes early in life and who did not experience institutionalization. These two groups of adolescents differed markedly in their intellectual and emotional make up. These differences were succinctly summarized by Goldfarb (1955) and recapitulated in an attempt to evolve some theoretical conceptualization of the findings.

Briefly, compared with the non-institutionalized children, those who were institutionalized exhibited:

1. greater mental (intellectual) retardation with special defect in conceptual ability,
2. an absence of "normal capacity for inhibition,"
3. hyperactivity, restlessness, unmanageability and difficulty in concentration,
4. superficial affectivity; indiscriminate seeking of affection, but with "no genuine attachments,"
5. absence of guilt feelings,
6. impairment or defect in social maturity.

These characteristics, considered as a syndrome, closely resemble psychopathic behavior disorders or descriptions of psychopathic personality.

It would, therefore, be quite relevant to ask if Kibbutz children, who to some extent experience Bowlby's "maternal deprivation" or Goldfarb's "psychologic deprivation," possess some of the character traits outlined above. To be sure, we emphasized that the Kibbutz experience is quite different from the stereotyped institutional experience. Yet, would this form of "discontinuous" mothering or multiple mothering and the relatively high child-adult ratio, as well as the frequently unpredictable gratification of tension that the Kibbutz child experiences, have *some* of the deleterious effects upon later personality development?

The studies just discussed are retrospective, for inferences regarding the effects of institutionalization are made from data obtained on older children (Goldfarb's adolescents). It is an indirect sort of evidence because the children were not examined *during* the period of deprivation or institutionalization.

Bowlby also gives a fairly detailed account of *direct* studies;

i.e., investigations of young children under conditions of institutionalization. The most general finding is that of developmental retardation, whether measured by a development or by an "intelligence" quotient. There is apparently a differential effect upon several aspects of development. Neuromuscular development, locomotion and manual or manipulative abilities are relatively little affected. Next come social responses which are somewhat more affected. Most retardation is noted in the area of speech, especially expressive speech.

If we were to address ourselves to the question posed above, i.e., "what are the effects of the 'partial deprivation' upon the children in the Kibbutz setting?" we would have to obtain information regarding the children at different age levels. Direct studies of Kibbutz infants and indirect, or retrospective, studies of older Kibbutz children would give us information that is parallel to that gained from studies of the institutionalized.

The impression may be gained that the evidence, concerning the effects of early deprivation on later personality development, is clear and unequivocal. Some studies, however, raise considerable doubt about the irreversibility of the process that presumably begins during the first three years of life as a consequence of psychologic and/or maternal deprivation.

A clinical follow-up study of "The effects of extreme deprivation in infancy and psychic structure in adolescence," by Beres and Obers (1950), provides us with very interesting data. Although the majority of the cases studied showed evidence of "psychic immaturity" as a result of their early experience(some were even psychotic and retarded), some exhibited "satisfactory adjustment." It is these exceptions to the rule that may make us ponder whether there are no flaws in the generalization. Moreover, Beres and Obers found that "by late adolescence about half of our cases have made some degree of favorable social adjustment."

Two important problems are posed by these findings:

1. The question of the inevitability of the deleterious effects of early deprivation upon later personality development; apparently the process does not take place in *all* instances.

2. The possibility that subsequent experiences may reverse the process or correct the "psychic immaturity" that presumably resulted from the earlier experience. Perhaps, as Beres and Obers speculate, "psychic structure is not immutably fixed," and flexibility in the years following infancy and capacity for further ego growth and development should be considered as a real possibility.

In the present context, the report by Freud and Dann (1951) on the group of children who were separated from their parents early in life (first year) and passed around from one place to another until they landed in a concentration camp (Tereszin) is quite relevant. Maternal deprivation and physical environmental deprivation were certainly characteristic of the early experience of these children, until they arrived in England during the fourth year of their life. Suffice it to say at this point—for we shall return to this study later on—that these children demonstrated a capacity for flexibility and for reversing the deprivation syndrome if, in fact, one actually had developed.

On the Consequences of Kibbutz Child Rearing

In the earlier section of this chapter, some of the clinical impressions of observers of Kibbutz children were briefly mentioned. Essentially the impressions were that Kibbutz preschool children exhibit a great many symptoms of emotional immaturity, such as thumbsucking, enuresis, and aggressive behavior. These, however, do not seem to persist, and subsequent development seems to be devoid of such indications of emotional maladjustment and neuroticism. In the judgment of the observers, the symptoms appeared with *higher frequency* than in like-age children reared in the ordinary family setting.

Two important issues may be raised in this connection. In the first place, do symptoms have the same meaning across cultures? In other words, are certain patterns of behavior that persist from earlier childhood periods universal, or equal, indicators of immaturity? Secondly, when we speak of "higher frequency" of occurrence of certain symptoms or immature patterns of behavior, the

57

assumption is that figures on comparative frequency are available. The fact is that symptom frequencies for unselected samples of children are hard to come by. Consequently, the clinical observer has to base his impression on his "private" rather than on available public norms.

It is to these issues that Kaffman (1961), who studied a group of 403 Kibbutz children (*all* children, aged one to twelve of three Kibbutzim), has addressed himself. He made a careful survey of the group of symptoms common in childhood disturbance in the Kibbutzim and compared the incidence with figures reported on larger samples in the United States. The main difference appears in the area of oral activity. In the Kibbutz, thumbsucking persists until about the tenth year of life with frequencies that are much higher than those reported for the United States. The opposite seems to be true for eating difficulties for which the frequencies are much higher for the American samples. The frequencies in a variety of other symptoms, such as enuresis, temper tantrums and aggressive behavior, did not yield any marked differences between the Kibbutz and non-Kibbutz children.

It is difficult to evaluate the effect of the permissive attitude of Kibbutz educators and parents in regard to the thumbsucking. Kaffman suggests that this attitude may be a factor in the greater frequency, although he does place considerable emphasis on early weaning as a source of early oral deprivation. It would appear that when more systematic methods of observation are employed, some of the clinical impression becomes questionable. Consideration of comparative norms and, possibly, differences in attitude toward certain kinds of childhood behavior, make the conclusions regarding the "maladjustment" of the Kibbutz preschooler rather vulnerable.

On the other hand, the positive aspects which characterize Caplan's (1954) impression of the older Kibbutz children are not unchallenged either. Caplan observed that the frequency of emotional disturbance among ten and eleven year olds is not greater in the Kibbutz than in Western society and that "as young adults they are remarkably non-neurotic." Yet Spiro (1958) characterizes the Kibbutz product of collective education as introverted, insolent,

58

hostile and insecure. Kardiner (1954), whose sources of information are hard to trace, speaks of them as "egocentric and envious, with little capacity for affective relationship, a good deal of mistrust and a good deal of mutual contempt."

These observations, for the most part unsystematic and uncontrolled, are difficult to reconcile with each other. The confusion cannot be unexpected; subjectivity, theoretical predilection and inadequate sampling contribute to it. It becomes necessary to attempt a systematic approach to the study of the Kibbutz child—his nature, adjustment and personality structure—along the temporal-developmental dimension. The subsequent chapters will be devoted to this broad objective. It is possible, however, from the vantage point of psychodynamic theory, to make *some* specific predictions.

PREDICTIONS FROM PSYCHODYNAMIC THEORY

Study of the effects of maternal or psychologic deprivation upon personality and ego development of the child is to some extent an indirect evaluation of principles emanating from psychoanalytic theory. The effects of the early infantile experience on subsequent development is a cardinal tenet of psychoanalysis. The outcome of inadequate object relationships, fixations as a result of excessive frustration at certain levels of psychosexual development, etc. are some of the psychodynamic processes implied when the consequences of early deprivation are evaluated. A number of specific predictions can be made as a result of the differences in the early interpersonal and intrafamilial relationships between the Kibbutz child and the child reared in the nuclear family setting.

First hypothesis. Toward the end of his discussion of the Oedipus complex, Fenichel (1945) refers to its relationship to the family structure: "If the institution of the family were to change, the pattern of the Oedipus complex would necessarily change also." Thus, the first question that might be asked of our Kibbutz data is with respect to the form of the Oedipus complex.

The Oedipus complex, described by Freud, is predicated on the patriarchal type of family in which the father is the dominant parent and supreme authority. In such families the father gains his status also by being the economic kingpin of the family unit; he is the provider, and the child is dependent upon him for his maintenance for many years of his life. The Kibbutz child rearing schema and its social structure has eliminated the authority of the father, nay, of both parents. As one Kibbutz educator puts it: "It is without doubt that the dissolution of the patriarchy within the Kibbutz decides in no small measure the relationship between the parents and the children" (Zohar, 1947).

There are several aspects of the situation that need to be spelled out. Since both mother and metapelet handle the infant, give him affection, and attend to his needs, the object relationship is not so intense, is more diffuse, and probably reduces the possibility of an exclusively eroticized relationship to either one of the maternal figures.

Although contacts with the father, in terms of time spent, are about the same as often encountered in Western society, the physical separation during most of the day and through the entire night reduces the possibility of viewing him as a competitor for the mother's affection.

With respect to the metapelet as a maternal figure and as a libidinal object, diffusion again appears to be the state of affairs. The lower intensity of object relationship in relation to this mother surrogate and the constant presence of several "siblings," competitors (members of the group) of whom the child may be jealous, bring about the lesser intensity of Oedipal feelings.

The lines of the classical triangle are very much blurred in the Kibbutz situation. The hypothesis we have stated on an earlier occasion (Rabin, 1957) that "Kibbutz-reared individuals will give less evidence of strong, but repressed, attachment to the opposite-sexed parent than persons reared in the conventional family setting" would therefore be justified and may be tested.

Second hypothesis. As a consequence of the modification of the Oedipal situation, differences in the identification process might be expected. Since the resolution of the Oedipus complex is said to take place via identification with the same sex parent, especially in boys, it may be asked whether the same formula pertains to the Kibbutz child. In attempting to answer this question, an examination of the components of the process is in order.

So that identification may take place, the following two conditions are necessary, consonant with psychoanalytic theory: 1) that the male child form a close and exclusive attachment to the mother or mother surrogate, and 2) that the father be viewed as a competitor for the mother's affection.

In the Kibbutz situation neither of these conditions clearly exists; the object relationships are more diffuse, and the attachment may be shared by mother and metapelet. Also, the father's position as a competitor for the affection of the mother (a less cathected object) is not as threatening as in the classical Oedipal situation.

Thus, a restatement of an earlier prediction (Rabin, 1957) is in order: "Kibbutz-reared individuals will evidence identification with the like sexed parent less consistently than will controls" (reared in the conventional family setting). A confirmation of more specific aspects of this hypothesis was reported in a previous publication (Rabin, 1958): "More boys, reared in the conventional family, will identify with the father figure, as compared with Kibbutz-reared boys whose identification objects will be more diffuse."

In view of the greater complexity of the Oedipus complex in girls, the prediction regarding their identification is not as clear-cut as in the case of boys. Nevertheless, the diffusion of identification should hold for Kibbutz girls as well.

Third hypothesis. This hypothesis is related to the different function of the parents in the socialization process of the child. Frustration of the growing child as a result of the demands made upon him by the parents (sphincter control, control of aggression, etc.) is an inevitable consequence of the child rearing process. The positive feelings of the toddler toward the parents combine with feelings of hostility. Thus, a state of ambivalence which, of course, is repressed, is part of the usual experience in the ordinary family.

In the collective education and child rearing of the Kibbutz, the socializing functions are for the most part in the hands of the metapelet who will be the target of a good deal of the child's hostility and ambivalent feelings. The hypothesis, therefore, may be stated as follows: Kibbutz children will evidence less ambivalence (or more clearly positive feelings) toward their parents than will children reared in the ordinary family setting.

Fourth hypothesis. The last hypothesis that we propose to draw from psychodynamic theory is concerned with sibling rivalry. Some of the relevant conditions in Kibbutz child rearing are as follows: 1) The child grows up with a group of "siblings" from earliest infancy. He does not find them, nor do they arrive at a later date (years after his birth) as in the ordinary family. There is no "dethronement" of the older child. Rather, early in his life, the Kibbutz child is forced to share the mother surrogate or metapelet; as an infant he is expected to work out a *modus vivendi.* 2) The *biological* siblings whom he meets during visiting hours may be viewed as competitors for parental attention and affection. However, this feeling of competition is reduced due to limited contact during short periods of time, and lesser intensity in the attachment to the biological parents. 3) The siblings as objects of displacement, as Oedipal objects, and as objects of hostility and ambivalence are not in the same position as in the ordinary family. This may be due to lesser intensity of both, Oedipal attachment and feelings of ambivalence (*see* the first and third hypotheses).

It appears reasonable to predict that "Kibbutz children will show less evidence of sibling rivalry than children reared in the conventional family" (Rabin, 1957). This prediction has received some support already (Rabin, 1958).

We shall briefly restate the four hypotheses which stem fairly directly from psychodynamic theory.

1. Kibbutz-reared children will give evidence of low Oedipal intensity.

2. The identification of Kibbutz children will be marked by a greater diffusion of objects.

3. Kibbutz children will exhibit little ambivalence toward their parents.

4. Sibling rivalry among Kibbutz children will not be intense.

Of course, in these hypotheses the baseline of the child reared in the "ordinary" family setting is implicit. All of the statements are comparative and in relation to children reared in the classical patriarchal type of family. It is not a matter of complete absence of certain qualities, but their different intensities in the psychodynamic process of personality development.

Some Additional Factors

Our discussion in this chapter was concerned with problems related to personality development of the Kibbutz child. We raised questions about the emotional, psychosexual and ego development—questions that might be subsumed under the general term of "character structure," and we anticipated some of the attributes of the emerging character. However, we have not referred to *content*, i.e., to some of the more specific attitudes that emerge with respect to a variety of situations. For example, we asked some questions about the *process* of identification (and by inference about superego and ego ideal), but have not concerned ourselves with the detailed contentual items that are obtained from the environment through identification and ego adaptation.

In our description of collective education, the importance of age groups or peer groups in Kibbutz youth society was highlighted. The age groups lead their autonomous existence, independently of other age groups and with minimal contacts with the adult world. As a result of these circumstances we have a situation of *role discontinuity*—termed by Eisenstadt (1950). Essentially this refers to the fact that Kibbutz children, in contradistinction to children brought up in typical agrarian societies, are isolated from the social and economic world of the adults. They do not participate in the economic pursuits and related problems of the adult members of the family because of the unique structure of the family in the Kibbutz. Neither do they assume responsibilities in the economic and social spheres in which adults are functioning. They do not "rehearse" so to speak, bit by bit, being an adult. The roles they assume are "age specific," discrete and noncontinuous with those of adults. It is not until late adolescence when they begin to work in the adult Kibbutz economy, that contacts with adults and initiation in their adult roles takes place.

What are the effects of such a discontinuity? If we are to accept the position that basic character structure is formed in the first few years of life when continuity with adult roles is least expected in any culture, then we should look for differences in attitudes of Kibbutz and non-Kibbutz children with respect to work, occupation and social and economic aspirations which are formed in later years and which may be most affected by differences along the role continuity-discontinuity polarities.

There are perhaps many additional experiences in the later life of the Kibbutz child that uniquely color his personality. The educational system, the ideology of the federation and its political orientation, and the values of the youth movement are undoubtedly of importance in drawing a complete portrait of the Kibbutz child. These issues are not our primary concern, nor can we make any specific predictions, but we may expect that light will be cast on these issues in the course of an investigation of the more structural aspects of personality development and emotional adjustment.

SUMMARY

The general question we are posing is: What is the Kibbutz-reared child like? The more specific areas for investigation that have been delineated are dictated to us by available data and theories concerning personality development deriving from experience in the nuclear family setting in Western society.

We have presented an analysis in which the institution and the family were compared with the Kibbutz on a number of aspects of child-adult interaction. Our conclusion was that in some respects the Kibbutz child is exposed to conditions similar to those described in institutions, whereas in others the similarity to the family setting is greater. As a consequence of this analysis, it was suggested that the Kibbutz child may experience "partial" maternal and psychologic deprivation. To what extent the personality that develops (following this degree of deprivation) has some of the characteristics of the "affectionless psychopathic personality," alleged to result from early deprivation, is a major question to which an answer will be sought.

In addition, consonant with psychodynamic and, more particularly, classical psychoanalytic theory, several specific predictions or hypotheses were evolved. We predicted that Kibbutz children, as a result of their early and unique intrafamilial and interpersonal experiences, will give evidence of low Oedipal intensity, little ambivalence toward their parents, sibling rivalry of low intensity and marked diffusion in objects of identification.

Finally, we will be interested in the effects of discontinuity of roles between child and adult in the Kibbutz, upon the children's attitudes to work, choice of occupation, and on a variety of other nonstructural personality "content" variables.

This limited assignment and the circumscribed objectives should be a first step in the direction of a more comprehensive understanding of the effects of Kibbutz child rearing on personality development.

4.

Research Strategy and Methodology

The questions concerning the product of Kibbutz child rearing, raised in the previous chapter, are of the kind that might be posed by intelligent parents and lay people in general, by curious educators, by the sophisticated clinicians and personality theorists. The research methods and strategy that were employed in the attack on these problems are the focus of the present chapter.

Psychological Research in the Kibbutz

Unlike the ethnographer or anthropologist, the psychologist, when investigating cultures different from his own, approaches his task with fairly specific expectations or hypotheses and with a number of techniques and methods for his armamentarium. "To carry on his field work, the anthropologist goes to the people he has selected to study, listening to their conversations, visiting their homes, attending their rites, observing their customary behavior, questioning them about their traditions as he probes their way of life to attain a rounded view of their culture or to analyze some special aspect of it. In this he is the ethnographer, the collector of data, which, in its wider ethnological significance, he will later, on his return from the field, analyze, and relate to other materials" (Herskovits, 1948, p. 79). Although many of the activities, listed in the quoted passage, were part of the present investigator's task, they served as a background rather than the focus of his undertaking. We may briefly mention some of the major differences between our task and that traditionally assumed by the anthropologist who had been engaged primarily in the investigation of illiterate (and so-called primitive) societies.

1. The Kibbutz society is highly literate and, primarily, of European origin.

2. It is a society within a society; a minority subculture within a larger majority culture which is not unified but diffuse because of its recent origins.

3. The culture or society which we investigated did not develop "organically" but on the basis of a conscious program, or blueprint, drawn up by its founders.

4. Our focus was not on the whole culture but on the relationship between children and adults as a basis for personality development.

5. We concentrated primarily on controlled observation and test methods rather than on episodic material and notations gathered by a participant observer.

Some of these differences were stated in a more expanded form elsewhere (Rabin, 1961).

We regarded Kibbutz society as a ready-made "laboratory" in which some of our ideas about the relationship of early childhood experience and later personality development may be tested. In order to perform the "experiment" adequately *controls* must be provided, i.e., subjects who live under conditions of the traditional family structure. Thus, our *independent variable*, the differences in child rearing and child-adult interaction, is defined by two different groups: Kibbutz and non-Kibbutz children. The *dependent* variable, of course, consists of the personality characteristics as elicited by means of our measures.

REPRESENTATIVENESS, SAMPLING AND CONTROLS

Before we describe the nature of the experimental and control samples, a word about representativeness is in order. The anthropologist may be satisfied to settle down in one particular village for a fairly long period of time and absorb his impressions, order them and collate them with other findings, and make generalizations about the "culture." Such a procedure may yield interesting, descriptive material. The generalizations may be valid since the society under scrutiny may consist of few units and may have a great deal of homogeneity stemming from long history and tradition. Some of these conditions do not hold for the Kibbutz society. The ethnic background, economic status and unique modifications of common practices make it questionable, if not hazardous, to generalize from one Kibbutz to all others. Consequently, we employed a *sampling* which was representative of Kibbutzim of different ages (from old to relatively new) and whose founders differ in origin and, perhaps, in cultural background (Russia, Poland, Germany, Hungary and the United States). Furthermore, since we decided beforehand which particular age groups of Kibbutz children we were to study, it was necessary to consider those villages whose children would meet the age specifications. For example, a young Kibbutz, in existence less than ten years, could not be expected to yield Kibbutz-reared adolescents. Similarly in a "middleaged" Kibbutz, young infants were hard to find; the founders no longer produced, and their own children for the most part were not old enough to be married.

We are now ready to return to the problem of controls. We could have decided to compare Kibbutz children with children reared in typical American families, but this would have introduced many additional variables. The findings might have reflected cultural differences in general rather than differences due to family structure and childhood experience. Consequently, we obtained controls from the broader Israeli society in which the typical, patriarchally oriented family is the rule. Thus, all our subjects had the broader culture in common. Language, geographic location, the background of the parents and the contents of the educational experience in the school were similar to both groups. The main difference *was* in the family structure and in the child rearing procedures.

For a number of reasons, which will become apparent, we selected the *Moshav* (pl. *Moshavim)* as the type of village most adequate as a source of control subjects. The Moshav is a cooperative type of settlement, but not a communal one like the Kibbutz. It consists of a group of individual land holders with similar amounts of acreage who, with the aid of the members of their own family, cultivate their land, raise crops, harvest and reap the profits. These farmers are hard-working and industrious and, in many ways, individualistic and even fiercely competitive. The major difference between this type of settlement and the usual village in Israel and in Europe lies in the extent of economic cooperation. Since agriculture is highly mechanized and the necessary equipment is too expensive for any individual farmer to invest in, the farm machinery is owned cooperatively. Moreover, consumption and marketing follow cooperative lines. There is group buying of consumers goods and organized, cooperative marketing of the products of the village economy. The family structure, however, remains untouched in the Moshav. The father is the head of the household and the mother is responsible for the children, taking care of the house and some auxiliary branch of the economy, such as raising chickens. The children, rather early in life, become members of the family unit economically as well as psychologically.

Aside from the contrast to Kibbutz child rearing that is presented by the Moshav family, there are many similarities between this type of village and the Kibbutz. They are both based primarily on an agricultural economy; there is also a good deal of similarity in the human material among the founders of both types of settlement. The similarities are in country of origin, educational level, idealism and in a great many of their national and political values and attitudes. It is also interesting to note that not an inconsiderable number of Moshav farmers and officials are former Kibbutz members. A sprinkling of children who spent some time in a Kibbutz may also be found in this type of settlement. Considering these similarities in the human element, there is a minimization of confounding variables when the consequences of different child rearing practices are the focus of investigation.

Some of the comparative aspects of the growing-up process in the Kibbutz and Moshav were discussed in the previous chapter in conjunction with the continuity-discontinuity of roles. A detailed sociological analysis of "Age groups and social structure—a comparison of some aspects of socialization in the cooperative and communal settlements of Israel" has been made by Eisenstadt (1950).

Some of the considerations that governed our selection of the several Kibbutzim for study were also important in the choice of Moshavim. Age of the Moshav, countries of origin of its founders and the degree of economic stability were some of the factors taken into account. The final selection resulted in the employment of subjects from eight different Kibbutzim and from four Moshavim.

THE NECESSARY CONTACTS

Obtaining the cooperation of the relevant authorities in the conduct of research of any kind, in any country and in any institution, is often a formidable task for the outsider. He needs to gain the confidence and trust of the leadership and convince them of the honesty of his intentions. This task becomes somewhat more complicated when dealing with the Kibbutzim. Aside from possible xenophobia, tinged by the socialistic political orientation of the Kibbutz movement, there is a good deal of sensitivity among the leadership of collective education about the critical scrutiny and appraisal of their "experiment" in child rearing. The caution with which outside investigators are regarded is reinforced by occasional *ex cathedra* pronouncements concerning the products of Kibbutz education which appear in the professional literature with which the educational leadership is well acquainted (e.g., Kardiner, 1954).

The plan of our research was presented at a joint meeting of the central educational committees of the two major Kibbutz federations. After some discussion and deliberation, and after discussion with individual members, the plan was approved and cooperation was assured. Letters of introduction to principals and teachers in the individual Kibbutzim facilitated the entry of the investigator, his selection of subjects and, generally, the cooperation of the local membership in the project.

Contacts with teachers, in the Moshav, who were former members of the Kibbutz were also facilitated by the original step described above. Subsequently, the cooperation of principals of the Moshav schools and the cooperation of the educational committees of the villages was also obtained. In addition, in order to obtain preschool subjects (infants) without going from house to house, acquaintance with the regional physicians and their assistants in the local infirmaries helped provide the necessary birthdate files and ultimately the collection of the appropriate data. Some of the details will come to light when we deal specifically with the several groups of subjects on which our study is based.

THE SAMPLES

A. Cross-sectional approach

Ideally, in order to study personality development as a function of certain variables, the longitudinal approach would be highly suitable. The optimal conditions would have been to be able to follow the development of the same children over a period of some 20 years—from infancy to maturity. The limitations of the life-span of the investigators themselves make longitudinal studies comparatively rare even in the United States. The tremendous expense involved would be an additional handicap. Such obstacles become multiplied when the investigation needs to be carried out far from the investigator's country of residence.

These, and many other, factors dictate the cross-sectional approach, i.e., the investigation of specific samples or cross sections along the age or temporal continuum. By studying groups of children at different age levels we can obtain a view of the developmental process of the children in a particular cultural setting. To be sure we do not study the *same* children at the different age levels. We assume that, by taking *samples*, the general characteristics of the older groups will be similar to those of younger children when they

71

reach the specific age under consideration; vice versa, the assumption would be that the older children studied were similar to the younger samples of the same culture when they were at their age.

The more specific question that arises is which age groups should be selected for examination. The ready answer might be: the age groups that may most clearly reveal differences, in the independent variables, between the experimental and control groups. The answer is unsatisfactory for it is difficult to find agreement on such points on the age continuum. Our own selection of cross-sectional age groups for investigation is justified to some extent on both theoretical and practical grounds.

1. Infants

In order to examine the possible effects of "partial deprivation" on the Kibbutz children we selected infancy as one of the crucial periods. Moreover, the Kibbutz infant between the ages of 10 and 18 months has undergone two important experiences—cessation of prolonged contacts with the biological mother as a part of the daily routine; and at least one change in metaplot. The children described by Spitz (1954) were separated from their mothers and placed in the Foundling Home at the age of three months. It is during the subsequent months that they developed the pathological symptoms he has enumerated. "These syndromes can be observed in their purest form during the period of infancy, that is, up to 18 months." Although the Kibbutz situation is markedly different, we thought that this period may be most important for the elicitation of differences and for comparison with a control group.

2. Ten year olds

The second group selected were fourth graders or ten year olds. This choice creates, perhaps, too much of a gap from the infant sample. We were interested in this group for two reasons. First, these children are at the end of the latency period and at the threshold of puberty. Their examination would give us an idea of how they have fared subsequent to the "deprivation" in infancy if that existed. Another reason, a practical one, is that at this age the armamentarium of conventional psychological techniques, many of them primarily verbal, would be suitable and easily employed. Nevertheless, it remains desirable to examine younger ages, at the preschool level in particular where a closer scrutiny of the effects of early socialization procedures may be possible. There are good reasons for the investigation of still other age groups. We shall have more to say on this point in Chapter 9.

3. Adolescents

Adolescence is generally regarded as the period of "storm and stress," the period during which there is a resurgence of many conflicts that lay dormant during latency. Since biosexual maturation is part of the definition of this period, age alone—especially the early teens—cannot be used as a criterion. Consequently, we selected the latter part of adolescence, chronologically, for then there is less likelihood of sexual immaturity. The groups of subjects, experimental and controls, were twelfth graders, 17 and 18 years old.

4. Young men

The three age groups mentioned above were included in the original design of our study. A supplementary group of subjects, consisting of young men only, became available. Since this group was older than our original groups, we seized upon the opportunity to obtain material on these men ranging in age from 18.5 to 21 years. It enabled us to get information about Kibbutz and non-Kibbutz children from *infancy to maturity*.

B. Representativeness

Once the age groupings were decided on, the task was to locate groups of children in the Kibbutzim (experimental) and in the Moshavim (controls) who would meet the age specifications. If any selection were to be made *within* any age group in any one village, then the question would arise to what extent the selected children were representative of all the members of that particular age group. The investigator was largely spared the process of selection within age groups. Since the age specifications of the groups covered a narrow range, *all* children of the villages contacted who met the age requirements became our subjects. Thus, by obtaining *entire populations* of specific age groups the problem of representativeness evaporates. This was the case for the infant and adolescent groups. The ten year olds were more numerous; consequently, a random method of selection was employed.

C. Description of the samples

1. *The infants* who were examined come from five different Kibbutzim and four Moshavim. Since the age range of 10 to 18 months was determined beforehand and since it is relatively narrow, all the infants who fell within that range were seen by the examiner. In addition, the parents and the metaplot were interviewed in order to obtain supplementary data concerning the earlier development of their charges.

Typically a brief visit and preliminary observation in the Kibbutz infant house preceded the actual examination of individual infants, some hours later or on the following day. This precaution did not turn out to be necessary for the children exhibited no fear or displeasure at the visit of a stranger. As a matter of fact, the most characteristic reaction was that of curiosity and interest. The infants were examined individually in a separate corner of the infant house or the sun porch. On one occasion, the conditions differed so the examination took place while two more children were present in the same large crib. Each child was ordinarily taken out of the crib and examined with the aid of the metapelet.

Upon checking the doctors' birthdate files in the two regional infirmaries which served the four Moshavim, we were able to select those children who met the age specifications. Invitations to bring the infants at a specified time were sent out by the regional physicians to the mothers whose infants' ages fell within the appropriate range. The vast majority of the mothers appeared at the scheduled time with the infants in their arms. They were present during the examination of their infants and occasionally assisted the examiner when such help became necessary. Two infants were not brought in;

one was ill and the other was away with the family on a trip. The mothers showed a great deal of interest in the examination, gave information, asked questions and were, generally, very cooperative. The examinations took place in the doctors' offices.

2. *The children's* groups in both types of settlement were more numerous. Originally we expected to confine ourselves to the fourth grade only, but the fact that there were consolidated fourth and fifth grades and that a fairly wide age range existed within the fourth grade expanded the age range of the subject samples to more than two years. The data (test findings) were obtained from six Kibbutzim and four Moshavim.

Ordinarily the procedure was as follows: All the fourth graders were given some group tests in their classrooms—usually in one session that lasted about one hour. At the close of the session the children were informed that some of them would be invited for individual sessions to the examiner's room. Every second child in the alphabetical list was "invited." Occasionally this random procedure was disturbed because the age of the child was outside the desired range. In the Kibbutzim, the examinations took place in the examiner's quarters which had been assigned to him by the Kibbutz educational committee. In the Moshavim the individual examinations were administered in one of the rooms available in the school building, such as a small library, a laboratory, etc. In one instance examinations were performed in a small museum. Privacy, however, was guaranteed and rarely disturbed.

The children, particularly from the Kibbutzim, were eager to be invited for individual examination and occasionally asked the examiner "will you invite me?" Sometimes they even pleaded to be selected.

As a consequence of the group and individual examinations this ten year old group yielded two samples: the sample proper, composed of children who were examined individually and the extended sample, consisting of all who took the group examinations.

3. *The adolescents* were drawn from the twelfth grade of four Kibbutzim and three Moshavim. The age range of these groups turned out to be comparatively narrow—a little over a year. More-

over, the overwhelming majority were between their 17th and 18th birthdays. A few subjects were younger.

Because of the relatively homogeneous age grouping of the founders of a Kibbutz (or a Moshav), some ages among the children are more prevalent than others. For example, young Kibbutzim have few if any adolescents; middle age Kibbutzim tend to have few infants; older Kibbutzim may show a bi-modal distribution—some adolescents and a great many infants who were born to Kibbutz-reared young couples.

At any rate, the settlements we sampled had relatively few twelfth graders. All of the twelfth graders in those settlements were examined both with group and individual techniques. Here, some attrition occurred. Some of the adolescents did not show up, for a variety of reasons, for individual examination. This was true for both Kibbutz and Moshav subjects. This attrition will be reflected in the tables reporting individual test findings.

The physical circumstances for the examinations with the adolescent groups were similar to those described for the "ten year old" sample.

4. *Army young men* constitute a fourth group. This supplementary sample became available through a happy circumstance. The present author was consulted on a research project conducted by the Officers Selection and Training Unit of the Israeli Army. This unit examines all officer candidates recommended to it from the ranks and advises as to final selection for officers training courses and officership. The unit employs a large battery of psychological tests as part of its screening and selection procedures. Some of the tests were the same or similar to the ones employed with our adolescent sample. The files of these young men for the year 1954 were made available, and the data on two parallel samples were obtained. From the files, 31 Kibbutz-reared officer candidates were pulled at random. Similarly, 31 files of candidates who were reared in ordinary Israeli villages and towns were obtained. The age range is approximately two and a half years—between 18.5 to 21.0 years of age, with an average of a little over 19 years. All subjects were *Sabras* (Israeli born).

Thus, we were able to extend our study to an age group that had left their Kibbutzim and their families and had been exposed to the broader spectrum of the Israeli populace. The test data, however, were not obtained by us, but were made available through the kindness of the appropriate authorities.

Table 4-1 summarizes the four different Kibbutz groups and the four control groups from non-Kibbutz settings as to sex, group location as well as the methods of investigation employed (to be described in the next section).

Table 4-1 Summary of subjects and materials on which the study is based

Group	N			Ages		Number of villages	Techniques employed
	M	F	T	Range	Mean		
Infants				Months			
Kibbutz	13	11	24	11.0-17.5	13.43	5	Griffiths scales
Non-Kibbutz	10	10	20	10.3-17.0	13.02	4	for infants; Vineland Social Maturity Scale
Children				Years			
Kibbutz	27	11	38 }	9.6-11.2	10.2	6	Rorschach; Blacky;
	(50	42	92)* }				Sentence completion;
Non-Kibbutz	21	13	34 }	9.2-11.2	10.2	4	Draw-a-person (Good-
	(24	21	45)* }				enough-Machover)
Adolescents							
Kibbutz	17	13	30	16.7-17.8	17.5	4	Rorschach; TAT;
Non-Kibbutz	14	11	25	16.7-17.9	17.6	3	Sentence completion
Young men							
Kibbutz	31	—	31	18.5-21.0	19.1	Various	TAT; Sentence Com-
Non-Kibbutz	31	—	31	18.5-21.0	19.3	Various	pletion; Question-naire

* Extended N

METHODS OF INVESTIGATION

Employment of standard techniques and testing methods enables the investigator to follow a systematic course in the comparison of his samples and in attempting answers to queries raised on theoretical grounds. It enables him to apply quantitative analyses to the data. Not all information obtained, even by means of standard methods, is amenable to quantification; this differs from technique to technique, as we shall see. However, the application of standard procedures is far more consonant with the experimental-quantitative approach than is the clinical-descriptive method.

Several major considerations had to be taken into account before a final selection of methods was made: 1) measuring devices suitable for the different *age levels* represented in the study had to be selected; 2) in order to address ourselves to some of the hypotheses raised in the previous chapter, we had to pick methods that would tap some of the relevant *psychodynamic variables*; 3) in order to reduce possible *errors* of translation and *"culture bound"* aspects of the techniques, methods involving a minimum of verbal stimulus material had to be chosen.

The test methods that we finally selected roughly fall in two broad categories: 1) *direct methods* involving direct questions, ratings and observations; 2) *indirect or projective methods* which facilitate the exploration of the fantasy productions of the subjects from which inferences about psychodynamic variables may be made.

The following paragraphs describe the several methods selected.

A. The Griffiths Mental Development Scale (1954)

This is essentially another "baby test" of the Gesell type, but of considerably later vintage. It is designed to test "intelligence" or mental development of infants during the first two years of life, and was standardized on a sizable sample of children within this age range. The scale consists of five sub-scales: locomotor, personal-social, hearing and speech, hand and eye development, and "performance." Since the last sub-scale required special equipment that was not available at the time of testing, the actual examination was confined to the first four scales. Descriptive statements about these four scales and sample items at the one year level follow.

1. *The locomotor scale* includes items which involve gross bodily movement and locomotion—from one place or position to another.

Many of these items, of course, form a part of many of the earlier infant tests. Example, "Can walk when led."

2. *The personal-social scale* "can give definite evidence of social adaptation." The items of this scale deal with the progress made in "personal-social learning"—the acquisition of customs and "mores" of his environment. Example: "Obeys simple requests: 'give me the cup.'"

3. *Hearing and speech* involves "active listening . . . (and) first vocabulary sounds." Example: "Says three clear words."

4. *Hand and eye* development refers to process of "assessing the child's level of manipulation." Example: "Can hold pencil as if to mark on paper."

The original full test, as mentioned, contains five factors, and its final scores and corresponding DQs (Developmental Quotients) are based on all five of the subscales. Our own final scores and DQs are based on a pro-rating of the four scales administered; i.e., we have multiplied the obtained scores by $5/4$.

In a detailed analysis of the data, the findings on the individual subscales and "group profiles" aid further in the evaluation of group differences. Such a procedure was followed in our study and is reported in Chapter 5.

B. The Vineland Social Maturity Scale

Unlike the Griffiths Scale which requires direct testing and observation of the infant, the Vineland Social Maturity Scale (Doll, 1946) is based entirely on reports and interview material obtained from persons most closely associated with the subjects. Scoring of the various items on the scale depends, therefore, on the information; the reliability and validity of the scores is dependent on this information. The relevant data were obtained from interviews primarily with the metaplot for Kibbutz infants, and from the mothers for the babies from the Moshavim (control group).

The Vineland is an age-scale which extends through maturity. However, we used it only with the infants for at the upper age levels many of the items are dependent on the cultural setting (United States) for which the method was devised and standardized. The items of the first two years are more "universal" and are applicable to the assessment of infant development in any cultural setting. A number of these items overlap with the conventional "baby tests," including the Griffiths, employed in the study. "Stands alone" or "Follows simple instructions" are examples of items that illustrate the duplication, at the one year level.

There are 17 items each at the one and two year levels. The scores on the Vineland scale yield a Social Maturity Age (SMA). A Social Maturity Quotient (SMQ) is computed in a manner similar to that of computing an IQ—by dividing the SMA by the CA (chronological age).

Although this instrument at the earlier age levels is similar to various developmental scales, it offers an additional dimension in the evaluation of the infants and is, to some extent, a check on the findings arrived at by a stranger (examiner) on the basis of a limited sample of behavior. The Vineland Scale measures "social competence" which, according to Doll (1953), is definable as "the functional ability of the human organism for exercising personal independence and social responsibility." In infancy, the first part of the definition comes close to that of a rudimentary ego.

C. The Draw-a-person technique

This method of evaluation was selected for two major reasons. First, it is a sample of nonverbal behavior which is particularly suitable for cross-cultural research; and, secondly, it is a versatile instrument for it possesses the potential of a psychometric tool as well as that of a projective device in the appraisal of certain personality attributes. It may also be added that it is intrinsically of interest to children of school age.

Machover's (1949) instructions to "draw a person" were given to all the children in all of the fourth grades, Kibbutz and non-Kibbutz, used in our study. The group administration method was employed, and ample time was given—until the last drawing in each class was completed. A pair of drawings, of a man and of a woman, was thus obtained from every child in the ten year old group. The material obtained was subsequently analyzed and used in the following ways:

1. *As an estimate of intelligence.* Several decades ago Goodenough (1926) set forth her method of "Measurement of intelligence by drawings." Her method is based on a detailed analysis of the characteristics of the drawings of "a man" which children were instructed to execute. The resulting Mental Ages and I.Q.s, based on the scoring system, showed fairly high correlations with standardized intelligence tests, such as the Stanford Binet. This method of appraisal of intelligence is particularly useful with children under the age of twelve, before specialized talent and training become factors of major importance in the production of the drawings. The estimate of intelligence was thus based on one drawing of each pair—that of a "man," in accordance with Goodenough's instructions.

2. *As a measure of "sexual differentiation."* When pairs of drawings, of a man and of a woman, are obtained, it is also possible, by means of a global evaluation, to achieve an estimate of the clarity of *sexual* differentiation reflected in them. This method has been applied to adults by Swensen (1955) who used a nine-point scale (for this purpose), ranging from "little or no sexual differentiation" to "excellent sexual differentiation."

We utilized Swensen's original five-point scale for the pairs of drawings: a) Little or no sexual differentiation—the two drawings are practically not different from each other; b) Poor sexual differentiation—some differences in length of hair and contours of body; c) Fair sexual differentiation—in addition to previous differences, some secondary sexual characteristics; d) Good sexual differentiation—clear differences in clothing, proportions and subtle facial characteristics; e) Excellent sexual differentiation—consistent differentiation on all items.

The descriptive material and samples for each category were used by two raters who achieved a high level of agreement in their ratings (about 94 percent). Swensen's original study (1955) reports a reliability of .84 for the scale.

The question may arise as to what the relationship is between level of sexual differentiation and intelligence as measured by the degree of complexity of the drawings themselves (Goodenough scores). A study reporting on sexual differentiation of American and Filipino children (Rabin & Limuaco, 1959) employed an analysis of covariance in order to investigate this very point—the possible dependence of position on the sexual differentiation scale on intelligence as measured by Goodenough. The conclusion was that "the findings obtained indicate that the differences with respect to degree of sexual differentiation cannot be accounted for by the differences on the Goodenough scores."

We limited our treatment of the drawings to the two indices described because they yield quantitative data for comparative purposes. More global judgments of a clinical nature may be made of the drawings. However, since such judgments are primarily qualitative evaluations which appear refractive to categorization, we refrained from reporting them. Some of the "impressions" will accompany the discussion of the quantitative findings.

D. Sentence completion techniques

Although the sentence completion technique is considered to be one of the projective methods, it varies considerably from some of the major ones along the directness-indirectness continuum. The stimuli, the sentence stems, are not ambiguous like a Rorschach inkblot, for example, and the respondent is usually more aware of the meaning of his response. The technique gives the subject more opportunity to exercise his defenses than do such methods as the Rorschach, TAT, and so on. Rotter (1951) states that "the purpose of the test is less disguised than other projective techniques." This may infer less depth and more defensiveness. Nevertheless, Rohde (1957) believes that the aim in using the sentence completion method "has been to elicit information from subconscious sources as well as from peripheral levels." Regardless of the level or "depth" of the psyche which is tapped by this method, an important advantage for our study is "that the sentence stems provide varied sets

and direct associations roughly along lines which can be prede-
termined by the investigator, even though permitting considerable
latitude of response" (Forer, 1960).

1. Forms for adolescents and children

A list of incomplete sentences by Sacks and Levy (1950),
although devised primarily for adults, appeared to be quite suitable
for our purpose in testing children and adolescents. The original
list contains 60 items which represent attitudes in 15 areas (four
sentences for each area). Of these 60 incomplete sentences we used
52 with the groups of adolescents, and 36 with the ten year old
children. The sentences employed (*see* the List) appear in a number
of instances somewhat modified from the original. These changes
are a function of the translation process. The original sentences
were translated into Hebrew, the language of our subjects. Translated back into English, they illustrate the imperfect equivalence of
sentences in different languages. We shall have more to say about
this problem later in this chapter.

SENTENCE COMPLETION

C	A	
1.	1.	I think that father only sometimes
2.	2.	When I have no hope to succeed
3.	3.	I always wanted
4.	4.	The future appears to me
	5.	My leaders
5.	6.	I know it is silly but I am afraid
6.	7.	In my opinion, a good friend should
	8.	When I was a small child
	9.	When I see a man and a woman together
7.	10.	In comparison with most families, mine
	11.	At work I get along best
8.	12.	My mother
9.	13.	If only I could forget the moment that I
10.	14.	If only my father were
11.	15.	I think that I have the capacity to

12.   16. I would be definitely satisfied if
13.   17. I hope
       18. In school my teachers
14.   19. Most of my friends do not know that I am afraid
15.   20. I don't like people who
       21. Before the war I
       22. I think that married life is
16.   23. My family treats me as if
       24. Those with whom I work
17.   25. My mother and I
18.   26. My greatest mistake was
19.   27. I wish that my father
20.   28. My greatest weakness is
21.   29. My secret ambition in life
22.   30. One of these days I
       31. (Omitted)
23.   32. If only I could be afraid no more
24.   33. The people I like best
       34. If I were small again
       35. If I had sexual relations
25.   36. Most families I know
       37. I like to work with people who
26.   38. I think that most mothers
27.   39. When I was younger I felt guilty about
28.   40. I think that my father
29.   41. When my luck is bad
30.   42. What I want most of life
31.   43. When I will be older
       44. People who I think are above me
32.   45. Because of my fears I sometimes have to
33.   46. When I'm not near them, my friends
       47. My clearest childhood memory
       48. My sex life
34.   49. When I was a small child my family
       50. People with whom I work are mostly
35.   51. I like my mother, but
36.   52. The worst thing that I did in my life

Beside the list of the incomplete sentences there are two columns of numbers labeled *C and A*. The *A* column consists of the consecutive numbering of the incomplete sentences administered to the

84

adolescent groups—from 1 to 52. The *C* column contains the equivalent numbers of the sentences of the children's form used with the ten year olds. These are numbered from 1 to 36.

A list of the *attitudes* tapped by this method follows. Since four incomplete sentences deal with each attitude, the adolescent samples were tapped for attitudes in 13 areas, whereas the children's test tapped nine areas.

	Attitudes tapped	*Item numbers*	
		Adolescents (A)	*Children (C)*
1.	Father:	1, 14, 27, 40	(1, 10, 19, 28)
2.	Own abilities:	2, 15, 28, 41	(2, 11, 20, 29)
3.	Goals:	3, 16, 29, 42	(3, 12, 21, 30)
4.	Future:	4, 17, 30, 43	(4, 13, 22, 31)
5.	Superiors at work or school:	5, 18, 31*, 44	
6.	Fears:	6, 19, 32, 45	(5, 14, 23, 32)
7.	Friends and acquaintances:	7, 20, 33, 46	(6, 15, 24, 33)
8.	Past:	8, 21, 34, 47	
9.	Heterosexual relationships:	9, 22, 35, 48	
10.	Family unit:	10, 23, 36, 49	(7, 16, 25, 34)
11.	Colleagues at work or school:	11, 24, 37, 50	
12.	Mother:	12, 25, 38, 51	(8, 17, 26, 35)
13.	Guilt feelings:	13, 26, 39, 52	(9, 18, 27, 36)

* omitted

The age level of the subjects was the major consideration in selecting the areas and corresponding incomplete sentence items. One item of the "superiors at work or school" category was omitted for it proved altogether unsuitable for the adolescents in the Kibbutz and non-Kibbutz settings. This is item 31—"When I see the boss coming."

2. Incomplete sentences of Army samples

The Army samples were not examined as part of the present project. Sentence completion tests were included in the psychological batteries administered, but, unfortunately, different forms were used at different times. Only twelve sentence stems were common to all forms. These comprise the sentence completion material on the Army groups. The twelve items are listed in Chapter 8.

No attempt will be made to categorize these incomplete sentences. Most of them seem to be concerned with the self-concept and self-appraisal under special conditions of stress. A few of the items are similar to the ones listed in the previous section. To a limited degree, study of the relationship of responses of the Army samples to those of the children and adolescents may be possible.

3. Methods of administration

There does not seem to be a uniformity of opinion with regard to the preferred method of administration of the sentence completion test. Our own procedure was governed by several practical considerations.

In the first place, in view of the fact that economy of time was imperative, group administration became necessary. Secondly, the age factor needed to be taken into account. Thus, the ten year old children were given mimeographed sheets on which the 36 incomplete sentences were reproduced, with ample space left for the completion of each sentence. The instructions, which were given orally by the examiner to each group, also appeared on the sheets so that the children could refer to them whenever necessary. No time limit was given, but everybody was finished by the end of the class period. There were, of course, considerable individual differences in the speed of completion—depending to a great extent upon the mastery of the reading and writing skills.

The procedure with the twelfth graders differed considerably. After the instructions were read, each sentence stem was presented orally, and a time limit of 15 seconds for the completion of each was allowed. Since these advanced high school students had no difficulty in writing, the time allowed for the completions seemed ample. We also reasoned that this procedure was preferable to no time limit, for it tends to reduce the possibility of reflection and excessive defensiveness. This rationale is not unlike the one that underlies the word association technique and is not altogether devoid of arguments to the contrary.

Oral administration of the sentence completion is also standard practice in the Israeli Army testing program. Consequently, this was the procedure that had been employed with the Army men from whose tests we extracted responses.

4. Scoring problems and procedures

In our treatment of the data obtained with this technique, we were not concerned, as were the authors of the test, with the formulation of a clinical judgment of each individual. Our concern was primarily with *group comparisons*, i.e., Kibbutz children versus non-Kibbutz children. One may rephrase this statement by pointing out that our approach was nomothetic rather than idiographic.

As a consequence of this aim, it became necessary to classify the individual responses (completions of sentences) obtained. The mode of classification or categorization, however, becomes a rather thorny problem. Investigators have often been concerned with the "adjustment" aspect of the responses. Although this is a worthy concern, even for the present study, we felt that a classification entirely based on the adjustment-maladjustment continuum would bypass the content and eliminate some of the flavor reflected in the responses. We resorted to a compromise solution by dichotomizing or trichotomizing the responses.

With the *father, mother* and *family* items we used the classification of positive and "other" (neutral plus negative responses). Thus, the response to item 8 (children's form) "My mother *is wonderful*" (italics indicating response or completion part) is classified as *positive*, while "My mother is 47 years old" is considered neutral and placed in the *"Other"* category.

The responses to items in the remaining attitude categories could not be classified in this simple fashion. It was necessary to examine the entire pool of responses to each incomplete sentence and evolve a set of categories appropriate to them. Preconceived categories would not work, for it is virtually impossible to predict the nature of the responses and the readiness with which they are classifiable into such categories. For reasons of simplicity and for the sake of statistical treatment of the findings, the number of response categories was either two or three for each item. The specific categories and appropriate examples will appear in the presentation of the results in subsequent chapters.

It may be pointed out that a fair degree of reliability in the classification of the responses was achieved. Two judges independently classified the responses with a resulting 92.5 percentage of agreement (Rabin, 1959).

In addition to the categorization of individual responses, a *global* evaluation of several attitude-areas was also undertaken. The procedure was to evaluate, or rate as positive or "other," all four items in the father, mother and family areas where the dichotomy was most meaningful and also was related to the questions raised in Chapter 3.

E. The Rorschach method

This most popular and durable projective technique requires no detailed description. Rorschach's ten inkblots were administered *individually* to the ten year olds and to the adolescents. Administration and scoring were in accordance with Beck's (1950) system.

Since the Rorschach scoring system contains a large number of variables, it was decided to select only those that may be considered relevant to the central problems of our study. The major scores considered for comparative purposes were those that are broadly related to what might be termed maturity, ego strength and ego control. (These scores are treated in detail in the results and need not be enumerated in the present context.)

A thematic analysis of the content of the Rorschach movement responses was also undertaken since these responses are assumed to reflect fantasied behavior. As a guide in categorizing the movement content we used Kaplan's (1954) method which is based on Murray's classification of needs.

Finally, "a measure of adjustment" based on 15 of the 17 "Signs of adjustment" employed by Davidson (1950) in her research with adolescents was also applied to our adolescent groups.

F. The Blacky pictures

In "A study of the psychoanalytic theory of psychosexual development" Blum (1949) introduced a new projective method—the

Blacky pictures. Since the publication of these pictures as a "test" (1950) the technique has been employed in a variety of clinical and research settings and has proved its usefulness in testing hypotheses, especially those generated from psychoanalytic theory.

The cartoon-like drawings of the pictures introduce a family of dogs—papa, mama, Blacky and Tippy. The suggested instructions for children, which have been used in our study, are as follows:

"I've got some cartoons to show you, like you see in the funny papers, and what I'd like you to do is to make up a story about each one. Here are the characters who will be in these cartoons (show frontpiece). Here (pointing) is Papa, Mama, Tippy, and the son, Blacky. Now for each picture I'd like you to tell me as much as you can about what's happening and what they are thinking and feeling. I'll leave this over here if you want to look at it later."

These instructions had to be slightly modified and adjusted to the cultural setting. Since "funny papers" is not a widespread Israeli phenomenon, the expression was not used. Also, the best equivalent for the word "cartoon" is the Hebrew for "funny picture," the term which was used. Reference was made to newspapers where such "funny pictures" do appear, even in Israel. We also had to cast about for equivalent dog names for Tippy and Blacky which are common, in a country where dogs themselves are not too common. In connection with the last point it may be noted that one Israeli psychologist doubted seriously whether dogs would even be adequate objects for identification for Israeli children. However, the actual testing and the results obtained dispelled all doubts regarding the stimulus potential for our subjects.

To return to the test proper, it consists of eleven cartoons in addition to the frontispiece. A brief description of the cartoons and the psychosexual dimensions they are designed to tap follows.

I. Showing Blacky in front of mother's nipple *(Oral eroticism)*
II. Shows Blacky with mother's collar in his mouth *(Oral sadism)*
III. Presents a series of four small "houses" with the name of one of the characters on each. Blacky is "relieving" himself between papa's and mama's houses *(Anal sadism)*

    IV. Blacky, near a bush, watching father and mother make love *(Oedipal intensity)*

    V. Blacky is licking himself *(Masturbation guilt)*

    VI. Tippy is shown blindfolded and a knife is about to cut off his tail. Blacky is watching *(Castration anxiety)*

    VII. Blacky, with his paw raised, as if reprimanding a small toy dog in front of him *(Positive identification)*

    VIII. Father and mother "making much" over Tippy who is seated between them. Blacky is watching *(Sibling rivalry)*

    IX. Blacky crouching and an apparition of an admonishing angel-dog is before him *(Guilt feelings)*

    X. Blacky is lying and a father-like dog appears in the dream *(Ego-ideal)*

    XI. Blacky is lying and a mother-like dog appears in his dream *(Love-object)*

The pictures were administered in individual sessions. In addition to the stories given in response to each cartoon, the structured inquiry for children, as suggested in the Manual of Instructions (Blum, 1950), was used. Many of the stories were rather unproductive, but the inquiry items which present a sort of "forced choice" situation, presented us with material that can be readily treated statistically. These specific responses can be related directly to stated hypotheses and predictions—a procedure which was in part reported in an earlier publication (Rabin, 1958). The inquiry questions about each cartoon will be listed in conjunction with the results on the ten year olds, in Chapter 6.

G. Thematic Apperception Test (TAT)

Among the projective devices in the clinician's and investigator's armamentarium, the TAT (Murray, 1943) holds a prominent position, is widely known and requires no detailed description. A few comments concerning its employment in our study are, however, in order.

1. Selection of cards

Administration of the entire series of 20 TAT pictures to each adolescent subject and their subsequent interpretation for both samples would have been a major project in itself. Since some cards are more productive than others, and some cards tend to offer the adolescent subject heroes for identification much more readily than others, we selected a limited number of pictures for administration. Such a procedure may be somewhat unorthodox in a clinical situation, but can amply be justified when followed in a research project and where the major objective is that of group comparisons.

The male adolescent subjects were given the following TAT cards: *1, 2, 3 BM, 4, 8 BM, 13 MF, 14,* and *17 BM.* The female adolescents, the following: *1, 2, 3 GF, 4, 10, 13 MF, 14,* and *18 GF.* TAT cards 4, 6 and 17 BM were the common denominator in the Army subjects' battery.

2. Administration

Although the TAT manual of instructions refers to individual administration only, there is sufficient evidence concerning the feasibility of group administration. Again, this is particularly defensible since the aim is not that of individual diagnosis but of group comparisons.

Subjects were given the standard instructions (emphasizing past, present and future aspects of their stories) and were asked to write down their stories. Testing was done in small groups—from four to six persons in each group. Each subject was given a card and instructed to take another when he had finished writing the story to the first one, and to continue until the series (of eight cards) was completed. An occasional question was answered individually. With this exception there was no further communication with the examiner nor with other members of the group until the testing period was terminated. Subjects were permitted to write as much as they wished about any one card and were free to leave the examining room upon completion of the task.

TAT material procured from the Army files had been obtained under similar conditions of test administration. The only difference was that in the Army the groups were somewhat larger, ranging from 12 to 20 subjects in each.

H. The Army questionnaire

Among the assessment methods employed by the Israeli Army for its prospective officers, a questionnaire about "conditions of work" and occupational choice was included. It is essentially a simple instrument of the multiple choice variety. As to occupational choice, each candidate was asked to name his preferred occupation. These occupations were subsequently placed into the following four broad general categories for purposes of comparison:

1. Military career
2. Agriculture—mechanics
3. Professional—artistic
4. "Kibbutz member"

Statistical Treatment of the Data

Of primary importance in the treatment of the data obtained are the statistical tests of significance between the groups with respect to the variables under consideration. Such tests lend strength to the findings and enhance their credibility, indicating whether the obtained differences are due to chance or reflect the fact that the populations are truly different on the dimensions under consideration. Statistical tests of significance, however, are determined by the sampling procedures employed and the types of tests or scales utilized.

Only the measures employed with the infant groups (the Griffiths and the Vineland) are classifiable as "interval scales" (Siegel, 1956) which are subject to parametric tests of significance. The Goodenough was treated in a similar fashion. With these measures the t test was used. With all other techniques employed in our study the nonparametric *chi square* was used as the test of significance Edwards, 1948).

With discrete scores or classifications, such as those resulting from the sentence completion test responses, from the TAT and the Blacky, the chi squares were computed from the contingency tables containing the incidence of dichotomized or trichotomized variables for the groups being compared. Although the several Rorschach variables are continuous, there is considerable doubt whether they are normally distributed. Hence, a nonparametric rather than a parametric statistical test would apply. In these instances we used the median test, which involves the frequencies above and below the median of the combined distribution of both samples (i.e. number of subjects in each group scoring above and below the combined median) in contingency tables from which the chi square value is obtained.

A level of significance of .05 or better was considered satisfactory for basing a conclusion regarding the comparisons between the groups. However, due to the fact that this is largely an exploratory study, levels of significance between the .10 and .05 will also be reported, for such findings may indicate *trends* which should not be completely discarded.

Generally, since no directional hypotheses were stated (the implied general hypothesis is that differences between the groups exist), a two-tail test of signficance was decided upon. However, in the few instances where specific, directional predictions were made on the basis of available and relevant dynamic theory, the one-tail test was used.

Adaptation of Methods to Language and Culture

In an earlier section, in connection with the sentence completion method, we have alluded to some translation problems involved in the adaptation of verbal testing methods from one language to another. We will amplify our comment on this problem and extend it to the adaptation of certain nonverbal methods (i.e., pictorial) for research in another culture.

There are two phases in the process of employing testing methods in a language in which they were not originally worded. First, the stimulus material and second, the responses obtained. Languages differ in structure, idiom and in many other factors so that an exact translation resulting in semantic equivalence of the material is hardly possible. Some modifications and approximations become a necessary part of the translation process. The Hebrew language, for example, has no neuter gender. Translations of such words as "people," "friends," "small child" which occur in our sentence completion test refer to the masculine gender, i.e., men (for people), male friends, and a small male child. This peculiarity may become a special problem to the female respondent; the attitude reflected by the little girl in the fourth grade may be to men in general, men-friends and little boys. This is but one illustration of the type of problem encountered. Many more could be enumerated. However, problems of translation of responses, especially to the more complex type of material, such as a TAT picture, are even more numerous. There is no doubt that many of the nuances of a TAT story are missed in the translation; the major variables, themas and dynamics can be teased out nevertheless.

The problems of the ethnographer who attempts to describe primitive cultures on the basis of scanty knowledge of the language and, often, through the medium of an interpreter are considerably different. The concern of Phillips (1960) with this issue and with the fact that "the question of translation procedures has often seemed wrapped in a conspiracy of silence," is quite justified. Modern Hebrew, however, is a modern language whose development and modifications have been under Western influences for quite some time; it is more readily adaptable to translation from English and to English. Moreover, we were not in need of an interpreter in our contacts with our subjects. This is not to deny, however, that absolute semantic equivalence is impossible to achieve.

An added aspect to be considered is the nature of the design of the present investigation. Comparisons are made within the same culture; responses of one Israeli group are compared with those of another Israeli group. Responses are not translated and then compared with a group that speaks the language into which the translation was made. If it had not been for the need for rating responses (by raters who did not know Hebrew) no translation would have been needed.

A few words about the cultural aspects of nonverbal stimuli may close this section. The visual stimuli to which responses are expected were the Rorschach inkblots, the TAT and Blacky pictures. There is no special problem, of course, with the Rorschach cards for the unstructured inkblots are not "culture bound." The TAT pictures by and large represent Western dress and figures—somewhat different from the persons one might meet in an Israeli village, but not different to the extent of dictating special redrawing of the pictures as Henry (1947) has done for Indians.

The Blacky, however, presented some interesting problems. In the first place, the rarity of dogs in Israel prompted a local psychologist to advise the investigator to use pictures of chickens instead; these are not a *rara avis* in the country and could be more readily understood. This warning, however, was not taken to heart, and the results justify our action. Young children, perhaps, could identify with animals of even a mythical nature. The second problem is one we encountered in the actual use of the Blacky pictures. It involves a common convention in the production of cartoons in the United States—the use of the balloon to denote speech or thought or imagery. Although Israeli children are familiar with cartoons to a certain extent, they are relatively unfamiliar with this type of convention, and the meaning of the balloons in the last Blacky pictures escaped a number of subjects. This fact had to be reckoned with when an analysis of the responses to the cards in question was made.

Many other problems, such as assigning to Blacky an equivalent neuter gender Hebrew name, etc., could be considered. But, they would not be so directly relevant to the findings of the investigation for their importance was relatively trivial, and their effects on the results inconsequential.

SUMMARY

An overview of the research design and the methods employed was presented in this chapter. *First,* some of the problems involved in doing research in the Israeli Kibbutzim were discussed. A comparison of the psychologist's task with that of the cultural anthropologist in the presentation of cross-cultural research was drawn. *Secondly,* the nature of the overall design was delineated. The major characteristic being that of a comparison of parallel age groups, Kibbutz and non-Kibbutz, within the same (Israeli) culture. Four age groups served as the basic samples upon which the investigation is founded. These groups were: one-year-old infants, ten-year-old children, 17-year-old adolescents, and 19- to 20-year-old Army men.

Procedures of random sampling or examination of "whole populations" meeting the age requirements governed the selection of subjects in the experimental (Kibbutz) and control (non-Kibbutz) groups. An attempt to construct a developmental picture by means of cross-sectional sampling is represented in this experimental design.

In the *third place*, the specific methods of examination or assessment at the different age levels were described. These were selected in order to explore overall personality differences between persons brought up in different familial and social settings as well as to test the specific hypotheses listed in the preceding chapter. With the infants, the Griffiths Mental Development Scale and the Vineland Social Maturity Scale were used to obtain an approximation of "intellectual" and ego development. With the pre-adolescent (ten-year-old) children the techniques employed were: the Goodenough (estimate of intelligence), the Blacky and Draw-a-Person (psychosexual development), the sentence completion (attitudes in several personality areas) and the Rorschach (adjustment and personality structure). The adolescents were given the sentence completion and selected TAT cards for the investigation of fantasy and personality dynamics. And, the TAT records as well as some sentence completion materials and data from a "work conditions" questionnaire were available on the samples of young men in the Israeli Army files.

In the *fourth place* the statistical procedures involved in the treatment of the data were briefly described. The statistical tests were parametric or non-parametric, depending on the nature of the data analyzed. Test scores that were normally distributed (as in the Griffiths, Vineland and Goodenough) facilitated the use of the parametric t test. In all other instances the median test (chi square) was deemed more applicable.

Finally, the linguistic and cultural problems involved in the translation and adaptation of standard assessment techniques involved in one culture and their application to another were briefly considered.

5.

Early Development:
Infants

Introduction

Two major methods of assessment of infant development were employed—the Vineland Social Maturity Scale and the Griffiths Mental Development Scale. These were described to some extent in the previous chapter.

In early infancy, there is a limited number of test items available on which test scales may be based. As a result there tends to be considerable overlapping between the different tests used with infants. The scales mentioned above are no exception. There is probably a high degree of correlation between them. The major difference is in the mode of obtaining information. The Vineland is based on information obtained from an adult *about the child*. On the other hand, the Griffiths depends on direct observation *of the child* himself.

The following pages contain a report of the quantitative results on both tests and a comparison of these findings for Kibbutz and non-Kibbutz infants. Some illustrative case material is then presented, followed by a discussion of the material and its implications as related to the differences in child-rearing practices.

Test Findings

A. The Vineland Social Maturity Scale

It may be recalled that Kibbutz and non-Kibbutz infants between the ages of 10 and 17.5 months were examined. The average ages of the two groups and the mean Social Maturity Quotients (based on the Vineland) are reported in Table 5-1.

Table 5-1 The two infant samples and the results on the Vineland Social Maturity Scale

	N	Age (months)		Vineland	
		Mean	S.D.	Mean quotient	S.D.
Kibbutz	24	13.43	1.54	98.7	9.9
Non-Kibbutz	20	13.02	2.04	106.1	11.4
Difference		.41		7.4	
t		N.S.		1.74	
P				.10-.05	

Vineland scores are readily convertible into Social Maturity Age (SMA) equivalents which are divided by the chronological age in order to obtain the quotient. As is the case with the IQ, the SMQ of 100 is considered average, i.e., there is a perfect congruence between the social maturity age and the biological age of the child.

We note from the table that the average ages of the Kibbutz and non-Kibbutz infants are very similar. The difference between the means is small and not significant statistically. The average magnitudes of the SMQ's of the two groups do differ. Although both means fall within the average range, there is a mean difference of 7.4 points between the groups in favor of the non-Kibbutz infants. This difference approaches statistical significance for the chances are only between 5 and 10 in one hundred that this is a chance difference.

It seems that fewer of the Kibbutz infants passed items at the upper levels of the second year on the Vineland scale. There is less frequency on passing such items involving some independence and attempts at mastery of the environment as "pulls off socks, transfers objects, overcomes simple obstacles, fetches or carries familiar objects." The trend is for the Kibbutz infants to fall behind the non-Kibbutz infants with respect to social maturity as measured by the Vineland scale. Both groups, however, fall in the average range without showing what may be called "retardation."

One qualifying statement is in order at this juncture. The sources of information differed from one sample to another. In the Kibbutz, the metapelet was the chief informant concerning the several children comprising her group of five to six infants. Informants concerning the non-Kibbutz children were their mothers. There may be considerable differences in the objectivity of the information obtained, for even infants whom "only a mother could love" may be described in a favorable light. Clinicians who have employed the Vineland attest to the major tendency of mothers to make their children appear better than they actually are. The informants are very ego-involved, and some of the Vineland items require the use of judgment which does not remain unaffected by emotional needs.

The metapelet, on the other hand, although devoted to her group of infants, does not have the same kind and degree of emotional investment as does the mother in her infant, in the conventional family setting. Hence, it is quite possible that the SMQ obtained for the Kibbutz infants is lower, partly, because the objectivity of the metapelet is greater and her interpretation of the questions asked, stricter than those of the ego-involved mother. This hypothesis might have been tenable if we had no checks on the results. As was mentioned earlier, the Griffiths, like other baby tests, overlaps on many items with the Vineland. Since this test is based on direct observation, it can serve as a check on the Vineland—to what extent the results are consistent or inconsistent with it. The Griffiths findings are, therefore, set forth in the next section.

B. Griffiths scales for infants

Findings with this scale tend to confirm the trend noted with the

Vineland. It may be recalled that the Griffiths is made up of five subscales; one of these scales was omitted in our testing, because the equipment necessary for this scale was not available to the examiner at that time. The general developmental quotient is, therefore, based on the scores on four subscales, converted into total scores (by multiplying by 5/4). Mean scores on each subscale and mean general quotients for both groups as well as the differences between the groups and the tests of significance appear in Table 5-2.

Table 5-2 Scores and general quotients based on the Griffiths Mental Development Scale

	A Locomotor	B Personal- social	C Hearing & speech	D Eye & hand	General quotient
Kibbutz	31.83	27.22	26.46	28.33	82.41
Non-Kibbutz	32.75	30.24	27.55	29.20	89.60
Difference	0.92	3.03	1.09	0.87	7.19
t	N.S.	2.88	N.S.	N.S.	3.09
P	—	< .01	—	—	.01

Several observations with respect to these results are in order.

1. On all the subscales the Kibbutz group scores lower than the non-Kibbutz group of infants.

2. The over-all developmental or general quotient which is based on the subscale scores follows, of course, the same direction, i.e., it is lower for the Kibbutz infants.

3. While differences on all subscales and the general quotient are present, only two of them are statistically significant—the differences on the "personal-social" scale and on the general quotient. The latter difference is, of course, not independent; it is to a large extent influenced by the results on the personal-social scale.

An examination of some of the items on each scale will illustrate wherein lie some of the major differences between the groups.

Very little difference is noted on the *locomotor* (scale A) scale.

Some of the items at the beginning of the second year level are: "climbs on a low ledge or step; stands alone; walks alone; kneels on floor or chair." It would appear that in the types of activities involving the larger muscles and navigation in space the Kibbutz and non-Kibbutz infants are developed at about the same level.

Most significant is the difference between the groups in the "personal-social" dimension. This subscale (B), according to Griffiths (1954), deals with "matters related to the child's personal-social learning, to his grasp of the *mores*, customs or folk-ways of his particular social group." Some of the items at about the one year level are: "waves byebye; obeys simple requests: 'give me cup,' etc.; and tries to help dressing." On this scale the non-Kibbutz group is markedly superior to the Kibbutz infants.

Differences on the C-scale (speech and hearing) again favor the non-Kibbutz group. However, these differences are not significant statistically. The contents of this scale are closely related to the social one. Both, active listening and pre-speech, involve a reaction to the immediate environment akin to the one assessed in the personal-social scale. Examples of items around the first year level are: "reacts to music vocally; babbles monologues when alone; tries definitely to sing."

Finally, the fourth scale (D) involves manipulation and "hand-eye coordination." Here, again, as on the locomotor scale, the differences between the infant groups are not very marked, although the direction is still in favor of the non-Kibbutz infants. "Can hold pencil as if to mark on paper; likes holding little toys; plays rolling ball" are some of the tasks that cluster around the one year level. Since these, as most of the items in all of the scales, depend on learning in the social context in addition to maturation, some gradations in their dependence upon social interaction may be discerned. The "hand and eye" scale, like the "locomotor" scale, partakes somewhat less of this social ingredient than do the other two scales.

In general, it is interesting to note that the composite Kibbutz pattern is: A-scale-high, B-scale-low, C-scale-low and D-scale-high. The non-Kibbutz pattern differs primarily in that B-scale is high in

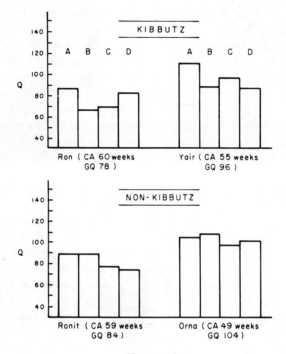

FIGURE 5–1

comparison with C which is also lowest for this group. The histograms (Figure 5-1) illustrate some of these patterns. The first two profiles are those of Kibbutz infants and the other two, of non-Kibbutz infants. The bars represent the values of the individual scales which have been converted into developmental quotients on the basis of the scores obtained.

In Ron's profile (first histogram) we note the general trend of the Kibbutz sample—the depression of the two middle scales (personal-social and hearing and speech) as compared with the two end scales. The second profile (Yair's) illustrates the fact that not all Kibbutz infants show exactly the same distribution on the several scales. However, the personal-social scale still remains depressed in this case also. The remaining two profiles, of non-Kibbutz infants,

102

illustrate the contrast. Neither for Ronit nor for Orna is scale B depressed. Also, the general scatter of subscale quotients seems to be narrower than in the Kibbutz profiles.

What meaning may be attributed to the group differences and the profiles just discussed? First we may turn to the originator of the test for relevant information. Subsequently we will relate the results to the nature of the experiences of our subjects in the two different child-rearing settings.

Griffiths (1954) states that "Maladjusted children show great divergence in their ability levels on different types of test. They tend to present a wide 'scatter' in the test results. Such divergences can be measured more accurately if dealt with in separate scales. Maladjusted children almost always drop in score on the Personal-Social scale and tend also to 'scatter' within this scale. . . . Failure on the Personal-Social scale almost always indicates some degree of emotional maladjustment. It suggests that the child is not learning, at the expected rate for his general ability level, those items of behavior that depend on his relations with his milieu" (p. 36). Later in the same volume the author considers differences in personal-social development which, in addition to maladjustment, are related to speech development as well. "These two are not altogether separate problems. A good personal-social development involves an out-going attitude to others which normally results in a conative trend toward speech, this being one of the functions of speech or pre-speech, an attempt to convey ideas to others according to the level of development. A poor or inhibited personal-social progress, such as may be found in cases of deprivation, naturally tends to result in an unwillingness or inability to try to communicate with others, and is likely therefore, to be associated with retarded speech development" (p. 90).

Although we do not have an objective measure of "scatter," we noted that this trend is present in the Kibbutz records. Statistical evidence for a lowering of the personal-social progress was presented. Hence, the issue of "maladjustment" may be seriously entertained. The next section contains some additional, relevant information on this point.

Brief Case Histories

Obtaining data for the Vineland involves interviewing of adults who have the appropriate information: mothers of the non-Kibbutz infants and the metaplot of the Kibbutz infants. Our interviews, however, went beyond the specific items required for scoring the Social Maturity Scale. The opportunity was exploited to obtain brief developmental histories of the infants in both groups. These interviews were not structured and the informants were encouraged to speak freely about the developmental progress of the children. Two such case histories of Kibbutz infants, selected at random, are hereby presented. The verbatim accounts of the metaplot were preserved and translated as closely as possible.

A. *Gadi* (Age: 14 months; DQ = 88)

"He is the third child in the family. The parents are very devoted to their children. They give as much love as it is possible to give. There is one sister, about eight or nine, who is a 'little mother'—quiet and serene. Gadi also has fine relations with an older brother who is in the Mosad. Mother is a worrier; exaggerates a bit. He is a sensitive child—a bit 'Quatch.' He wants everyone to kiss him and embrace him. He was nursed a lot; he had about eight and a half to nine months. Transferred to artificial food nicely. Passed from mother to metaplet—after weaning—without difficulty. It was a gradual weaning. Afterwards the mother just did not appear at feeding time. He felt the separation for about two or three weeks. Now he is all right.

"Gadi generally sleeps well. Occasionally there are disturbances at night; he lies awake or he 'talks' in his sleep. He can cry for hours and be very unhappy because of a small wound or accident. He was ill, with a very high temperature (no diagnosis). When he falls he sometimes lies there—some special weakness of the muscles. He had episodes of falling and lying unconscious, rolling his eyes— for only seconds. Now there have not been such episodes for three months. He cries a lot during the night—since his illness.

"Gadi eats well and with great gusto; with his hands. He throws himself down on the floor when he does not wish to eat. Usually he eats fine; loves to eat pieces—solids; loves to drink a lot.

"There are no conflicts between him and the other children in the group. He is the smallest. For months he did not play at all. At the age of nine to ten months he began to play. He was not interested in toys and put everything in his mouth. He shows more interest in the motion of people than in toys."

B. *Ofrah* (Age: 13½ months; DQ = 75)

"This child was not born in the hospital; she was suddenly delivered at home. She was given more than usual care. Ofrah is the second daughter of a young couple. The older sister who is about five is quite pampered—'she turns their head' (the parents').

"She was nursed from the start—until she was five months old. She was very quiet; her presence was hardly felt in the nursery room. We didn't know at all that she had a voice. She ate and slept quietly all the time. An unusual 'angel' was lying there.

"Suddenly when she was about seven months old she 'woke up.' I don't know what happened to her but she started to be a hysterical child. She jumps up, vomits three times a day, etc; cries all the time.

"When she was being weaned, the mother came down with whooping cough. The mother would not enter the nursery but would come daily to the window. This would upset the child terribly. Vomiting would follow. It seemed deliberate. She wouldn't vomit when the metapelet would say—'no, Ofrah, I don't want you to do that!' Perhaps I reacted too much at that time. This was during the period when the mother was absent. When the mother started coming again (Ofrah was eight months old then), the situation was all right when she was with me. With her mother, she transferred all the tricks that she had tried with me.

"The older child, the five year old, hates Ofrah ("If she gets sick, when will she die?' etc.). She has trouble leaving the parents evenings and acts up before returning to the children's home after the daily visit.

"Ofrah stays awake for hours at night. During the last few months she tends to be awake during the second half of the night.

"The first word she said was 'Daddy'; the second was 'Leah' (the name of the metapelet). She loves children and likes to be with them and play with them. She does not like adults.

"Weaning was a real crisis for her. Her difficulties started around that time. She is a poor eater; eats solids with difficulty. She also causes the parents plenty of trouble; in the evenings especially (separation!) She is a thumb sucker and sucks a lot.

"In general—development was slow; everything appeared late. Her teeth did not appear until she was a year old."

These brief descriptions of two infants bring into focus several issues that are relevant to a possible explanation of the relative retardation in the development of the Kibbutz infants. It seems that the first several months of life pass uneventfully. Development seems to be normal in most respects. However, following the weaning period there seem to be some severe reactions. In the case of Gadi the described episodes of unconsciousness may have an organic origin (high temperature)—possibly some sequelae of a form of encephalitis which has not been diagnosed as such. However, his excessive craving for affection, over-reaction to physical injury and the sleep difficulties would seem to have a more psychogenic than organic basis. In most respects, Gadi does not seem to exhibit severe signs of maladjustment. He eats well, plays adequately and maintains good peer relationships.

Ofrah's life history appears to be a bit more complicated. Although she was born somewhat unexpectedly (at home), she was not a premature baby. Early development appears to be normal, although she was probably too much of an "angel." Here again, when she was seven months two important events took place; one—the usual weaning; and the other one—the tantalizing and traumatic experience of seeing the mother (through the window), but not being with her. The vomiting, crying and jumpiness followed. The sleeping difficulties at night (lying "awake for hours") further complicate the picture. Here the symptoms are all apparently of a psychogenic nature and would readily classify the child as "maladjusted."

These two infants are by no means atypical for the Kibbutz group, whereas the infants in the control group are in most instances free of this type of behavior. We see that the comments quoted with regard to the developmental patterns on the Griffiths and their relationship to "maladjustment" are applicable to a degree. Not only has there been an overall lag in the development of the Kibbutz infants as attested by the relatively low developmental quotients, but the selectivity of the functions affected (personal-social) seems to have some special meaning in terms of unevenness in the developmental process.

The possible causes for the differences in the developmental pattern need to be sought in the differences of the infantile experience which is embedded in the two types of child-rearing practices. An attempt to pinpoint some of these differences and relate the findings to them will be made in the section that follows.

Discussion

In explaining the results obtained with the infant samples, the first task is to review briefly the major differences in the experiences of the Kibbutz and non-Kibbutz child during the first year and a half of his life. These differences are especially in the area of interpersonal relationships, for with respect to health, nutrition and physical care the differences are not substantial. Even these factors, however, may be affected by the interpersonal interaction.

From the very beginning the Kibbutz infant is subjected to *multiple, or concomitant, mothering.*

First, the biological mother is available for all feedings during the first months of life. Her presence, however, is *not continuous;* she is not readily available to the infant during the periods between feedings. During those times she may be back in her quarters and later, after the first six months or so, at work.

Second, the metapelet in charge of the infant house is available most of the day; she is at the "beck and call" of the infant when the mother is not around. (But several other infants also may make demands upon her time and services.)

Third, still another adult is introduced in the person of the metapelet's assistant; especially in the afternoon, when the regular metapelet takes time off for a rest and to attend to her own family affairs.

Fourth,—the night watchwoman. Here is another adult who responds to emergencies at night when neither mother or metapelet, or her assistant, are available to the infant. It is this watchwoman, assigned to the entire complex of infant, toddler and children's houses, who responds when the infant cries or is restless. Often the response is not immediate, especially in Kibbutzim where there is a considerable geographic dispersal of the various children's houses. The importance of this adult must not be underrated, however, for she oftentimes fulfills a crucial need in the dark of the night.

After the first several months, the role of the mother and the amount of contact with her infant diminishes. At the same time, the role of the metapelet becomes increasingly important. She begins to take over the feeding functions and is more continuously with the infant. By the time the infant is nine months old, his contacts with the mother become reduced to the afternoon and holiday visits in the company of the rest of the family. The roles of the assistant and the night watchwoman remain constant and subsidiary.

Fifth, another factor must be considered—the change in meta-plot. The metapelet who was with the infants during the first nine months or so, usually relinquishes her charges to a new metapelet who takes over for the next few years. Thus, in addition to the multiple mothering, *separation* from the first metapelet takes place and adjustment to a new one becomes necessary all before the infant is one year old.

What does it all mean to the young infant? To reconstruct "meaning" for the infant is a hazardous undertaking. We do not have reports from the infants regarding their experiences, but we must *infer* and speculate consistently within a theoretical psycho-dynamic framework.

It would be fair to state that the Kibbutz infant experiences more frustration in the fullfilment of his needs than the infant in the standard family setting. In the first place, a good deal of the time—day and night—the response of the adult to his needs is not immediate and "magical." Second, the care and handling differs from adult to adult; there is no stability and security with respect to the *mode* in which the care is exercised. These frustrations are probably more than the infantile ego can readily adjust to and handle or integrate. Some disturbance in the orderly process of ego development during this period must occur, a disturbance reflected in our test findings.

It is of importance, however, to point out that in the Kibbutz setting we are dealing neither with maternal deprivation nor with separation in the sense discussed in Bowlby's monograph (1951). The relationship of the mother to the infant is highly personal, marked by a great deal of affection and warmth. Yet, it is different, for the intervals between contacts are longer than in the ordinary family; by the end of the first year affection is "rationed," to be had during the visiting hours primarily. The contacts with the mother are continuous, but perhaps lacking in constancy; by the middle of the first year, the contacts with the metapelet become constant, but lack in continuity for she is replaced before the year is over by another. Thus, it depends on our definition of continuity of mother-child relationships whether the Kibbutz infant's experience can be characterized as continuous. On the other hand, the term "maternal deprivation" does not fit either. Our results are not the same as those obtained by Spitz (1946); the term "hospitalism" cannot be applied to the Kibbutz infants. Still, the test results do show that some retardation and unevenness in the development do occur.

Other, related factors should not be neglected. As we stated on another occasion: "It may be that the early retardation noted in our findings is due to the comparatively high child-adult ratio in early infancy, rather than to the intermittency of mothering" (Rabin, 1958, p. 583). The infant begins rather early with multiple object relationships. His maturation is not yet adequate, the task is overwhelming so that the resulting frustration and anxiety precipitate a partial withdrawal which hinders the infant's development, especially in the personal-social sphere.

Two more points with respect to the nature of the testing instrument must be made before closing the chapter. First, Table 5-2 which lists the mean developmental quotients for both groups discloses that both are below the average level. This, no doubt, reflects the fact that the Griffiths scales were standardized in a different culture (Great Britain) and may not be perfectly suitable for the assessment of infant development in another culture. Some "culture-bound" items could be readily pointed out. The use, however, we made of the scales, for comparative purposes, is justified for groups within the same culture.

The second point is with reference to the purpose for which "baby tests" may be used. Their employment in the assessment of current development during infancy is justified. This, however, does not imply their predictive value for future development. Bayley's (1955) comment is quite pertinent in this connection. "So far none of these efforts has been successful in devising an intelligence scale applicable to children under two years that will predict their later performance" (p. 807). The material to be presented in the subsequent chapters will further reinforce this conclusion.

Summary

Kibbutz and non-Kibbutz infants between the ages of 10 and 17 months were compared on social maturity and general development by means of the Vineland Social Maturity Scale and the Griffiths Mental Development Scale respectively. The findings indicate the superiority of the non-Kibbutz over the Kibbutz group on both measures. Especially noteworthy is the differential lag of the Kibbutz group on the personal-social scale of the Griffiths test; to a lesser extent the speech and hearing dimension is similarly affected. Two randomly selected case histories of Kibbutz infants were presented indicating some of the emotional maladjustment difficulties apparently characteristic of this group, paralleling the characteristics of the profiles of the subscale distributions.

Discussing the data in the light of the differential experience of Kibbutz infants as compared with those in the ordinary family setting, some explanatory hypotheses were suggested.

1. Kibbutz infants experience multiple mothering and diffuse early object relations which are frustrating and anxiety provoking to the budding ego and cause a degree of withdrawal from interpersonal relations.

2. This withdrawal tends to reduce identification and interferes

110

with the orderly learning and developmental process which becomes reflected in lower achievement, especially in the personal-social sphere which is most likely to be affected by withdrawal.

3. A high child-adult ratio—limited contacts with adults and older siblings—further reduces learning and imitative opportunities needed for development of speech skills.

Limitations of the value of absolute scores on a scale standardized in one culture and applied in another were briefly noted. The inadequacy of infant scales in predicting later mental development was emphasized.

6.

Preadolescence: The Ten Year Olds

By far the largest group of children in the present study were the fourth graders, ranging in age between nine and eleven years, with a median age of about ten years. The groups could be described as constituted of children at the end of the latency period and at the beginning of preadolescence and prepuberty. Our main concern was whether the lag in development, noted in Kibbutz infants, tends to persist through later ages; we were also interested in the personality make-up of these children—its structure, dynamics and specific fantasy content. The concern was with attitudes relatively close to consciousness as well as with personality dynamics not so readily available to awareness and not so readily sifted and controlled by ego-defensive processes.

As a consequence of the broad objectives that we set for ourselves a number of different methods of study and assessment were employed. These methods permit the drawing of inferences concerning different levels of functioning. The results will first be described in this chapter for each specific technique. Subsequently, the findings under each test will be related to those of the others in an attempt to observe congruities or incongruities between them. This procedure will finally lead us to our conclusions about the Kibbutz children vis-a-vis the control non-Kibbutz group.

THE DRAWINGS

It will be recalled (Chapter 4) that all the ten year old children drew "a person" and then "a person of the opposite sex." These drawings were essentially utilized for two purposes—as a Goodenough test (1926) for the estimation of intellectual functioning and as a method of assessing sexual differentiation.

A. Index of intelligence

For more than thirty years Goodenough's (1926) method of assessing intelligence by means of the draw-a-man test has been widely used. The results have generally correlated quite well with standardized tests such as the Stanford-Binet and others. The viability and usefulness of this method in particular, and of the study of children's drawings in general, are attested by the extensive literature available (Goodenough & Harris, 1950).

This method was used with groups of children in their classrooms. Groups of 40 children from the Kibbutz and non-Kibbutz samples were compared in order to minimize the age differences and variations. The male drawings of each pair of drawings obtained were scored by the Goodenough method and equivalent MA's (mental age) were thus arrived at. Subsequently the IQ's for all the children were calculated by the usual method (dividing the MA by the chronological age and multiplying by 100). A summary of the results is presented in Table 6-1.

Table 6-1 Comparison of Goodenough IQ averages

	Number of villages	N	CA in years		IQ		
			M	Range	M	Range	S.D.
Kibbutz	6	40	10.25	9.6-11.3	99.70	61-134	16.71
Non-Kibbutz	4	40	10.13	9.2-11.3	92.70	59-136	19.07
Difference					7.00		
P					.10-.05		

It can be readily noted that there are no significant differences in average age and range of ages between the two groups. They are pretty well matched in this respect. Although the IQ ranges are about the same, the averages differ considerably; the difference, however, does not quite reach statistical significance. The average IQ of the Kibbutz children is 99.70—approaching the ideal average, for a random sample of children, which is an IQ of 100. Non-Kibbutz children achieved an average which is seven IQ points below that of the Kibbutz group, although still classifiable within the average category. The evidence tends to point to a higher level of intellectual development of the Kibbutz children, pending corroboration of the evidence from additional sources.

B. Sexual differentiation

Since the children drew a male and a female figure the Scale for Sexual Differentiation could be applied. As indicated earlier, we employed an adaptation of Swensen's (1955) nine-point scale. The main underlying assumption is that the drawings project the awareness of and concern with the differences between the sexes on the part of the subject.

A global kind of judgment is involved with some aid obtained from the samples supplied by Swensen. Levels of differentiation range from "little or no sexual differentiation" to "excellent differentiation." In the former case the drawings are practically *asexual* involving similarity in body structure, clothing and features; in the latter case there is evidence of differences in the several areas (including secondary sexual characteristics), and the drawings are perfectly distinguishable from each other.

Two judges evaluated the drawings independently, placing them finally in four categories, ranging from poor to excellent differentiation. Agreement between the judges was originally reached in 92.5 percent of the cases. Disagreements involved the use of neighboring categories. Following discussion, agreement was reached on 7.5 percent of the cases. Following this, the two higher and two lower categories were combined, and the data were dichotomized into "high" sexual differentiation (categories 3 and 4) and "low" sexual differentiation (categories 1 and 2), in order to facilitate statistical treatment.

The data to be presented are based on all of the *pairs of drawings* that were obtained from the Kibbutz and non-Kibbutz fourth graders. (Some of the drawings were discarded either because one of the figures was incomplete or not drawn at all.) Thus, 82 pairs of drawings of Kibbutz children and 46 of non-Kibbutz children were evaluated with respect to degree of sexual differentiation.

Since the method of evaluation we employed had not been used much in the United States (and for reasons that will become clearer later), we included a sample of fourth graders from American schools, composed of 45 children, about evenly divided between boys and girls. Table 6-2 lists the numbers in each group and reports the incidence of the pairs of drawings in the two major categories of sexual differentiation.

Table 6-2 Distribution of the drawings of the three groups in dichotomized categories of sexual differentiation

Categories	Kibbutz			Non-Kibbutz			United States		
	M	F	T	M	F	T	M	F	T
1 & 2 (low)	24	17	41	10	5	15	12	5	17
3 & 4 (high)	23	18	41	10	21	31	16	12	28
	47	35	82	20	26	46	28	17	45

Examination of the table quickly reveals the major trend: the Kibbutz children are equally divided between the two categories, while the non-Kibbutz and American children show a relatively low incidence in the "low" category, with the majority falling in the "high" category.

Application of the chi square test to the observed differences yields some significant results. When the total Kibbutz sample is compared with the non-Kibbutz children the chi square value approaches significance, i.e., it is close to the .05 level of confidence. The differences between the Kibbutz and the U.S. children are even more marked and are statistically significant. A comparison of the non-Kibbutz with the U.S. sample yields no significant differences whatsoever. The conclusion that both family-oriented samples (non-

115

Kibbutz and U.S.) are superior to the Kibbutz sample on the sexual differentiation dimension is inescapable.

Table 6-3 Chi square values for the differences between the groups and between the sexes in each group on the levels of sexual differentiation

Comparison of groups	Chi^2	Comparison of sexes within groups (M vs. F)	Chi^2
Kibbutz vs. Non-Kibbutz	3.58*	Kibbutz	0.09
Kibbutz vs. U.S.	5.03**	Non-Kibbutz	4.93**
Non-Kibbutz vs. U.S.	0.05	United States	3.69*

*P = .06   **P = .03-.02

Chi square values for the differences between the sexes *within* each group reveals some further interesting differences. Again the non-Kibbutz and U.S. samples show a similar tendency which differs from the one noted in the Kibbutz group. Girls in the former samples show superiority to the boys in the area of sexual differentiation, whereas there are no differences between the boys and girls of the Kibbutzim in this respect. It would appear, moreover, that the girls of the non-Kibbutz and the U.S. groups are responsible for the over-all differences between these groups and the Kibbutz children. (*See* Table 6-3).

Apparently awareness of sexual differentiation is more acute among the pre-pubescent girls reared in the ordinary family setting than is the case with the Kibbutz girls, who are similar to the boys in this respect. A further test of the significance of the differences between the girls' groups would show both non-Kibbutz groups considerably different (P values beyond .05 level) than the Kibbutz girls. No such differences between the boys' groups are obtainable.

As we pointed out in the earlier discussion of the sexual differentiation scale (in Chapter 4), an analysis of covariance indicated the independence of this measurement from intelligence and general quality and complexity of the drawings as measured by Goodenough's method (Rabin & Limuaco, 1959). Furthermore, in the previous section of the present chapter we reported the relative superiority of the Kibbutz children on the Goodenough (intelligence) scale. Thus, the measure of sexual differentiation may be treated and considered as relatively independent of intelligence and drawing complexity.

C. Summary

Two indices were obtained from the draw-a-person technique. First, the male drawings were scored according to Goodenough's method; the scores served as the basis for obtaining the MAs and corresponding IQs for the subjects. Second, the pairs of drawings were rated as regards sexual differentiation.

1. A comparison of the mean IQs of the Kibbutz and non-Kibbutz groups indicates the superiority of the former group. The differences between the groups approaches statistical significance.

2. Non-Kibbutz and American fourth graders achieve higher levels of sexual differentiation than do Kibbutz children.

3. There are no differences in the incidence of high and low levels of sexual differentiation between the non-Kibbutz and the American sample.

4. Girls are superior to boys on the measure of sexual differentiation in the non-Kibbutz and American samples; Kibbutz girls do not differ in this respect from Kibbutz boys.

5. The over-all group differences between children reared in the ordinary family setting (both control groups—Israeli and American) and the Kibbutz children are actually due to the superiority of the girls in the former and to achievement similar to that of the boys in the latter; i.e., the real difference is between the girls and not between the total samples.

RORSCHACH METHOD

Rorschach's inkblots have figured in literally thousands of investigations. The number of ways in which the data have been treated is legion, and the investigator who employs this method must make a decision, perhaps an arbitrary one, as to what he is to look for in the projective material obtained from his subjects. To be sure, detailed personality descriptions, such as those included in some clinical-anthropological studies, could be presented. However, the problem of quantification of such data, for we are concerned with group comparisons, is nigh insurmountable. Consequently we settled on the study and comparison of a number of conventional indices and determinants, especially those related to intelligence and ego development, as well as on certain indices and global judgments of maturity and adjustment reflected in the test findings. One of our concerns was to deal with some of the variables reported by Goldfarb (1944) on older children with different types of experiences in institutions and adoptive homes. These will be referred to more specifically in the over-all discussion of the Rorschach results at the close of the present section.

Our study is based on a total of 72 records. Of these, 38 are of Kibbutz children and 34 of non-Kibbutz ten year olds. There are 27 boys and 11 girls in the first group and 21 boys and 13 girls in the non-Kibbutz group.

A. Indices of intelligence and ego development

In selecting Rorschach variables that are related to intellectual functioning we followed Beck (1950) for the most part. Most of the nine dimensions which we employed did not show marked differences between the groups. On three of the variables the differences are significant or approach statistical significance. First, accuracy of perception—an important ingredient of intelligence and an indicator of ego development—is significantly higher for the Kibbutz group. Second, the Kibbutz youngsters tend to emphasize small details in their perception; this points to the quality of the intellectual approach rather than the level of intelligence *per se*. Third, the breadth and range of content in the responses favors the Kibbutz children. Greater extensiveness of cultural background may be noted as well as an ability to take advantage of this background; it is readily available in the associational "stream of consciousness." The detailed statistical findings have been reported elsewhere (Rabin, 1957b, 1958a).

B. Significant ratios and determinants

A multidimensional instrument such as the Rorschach can yield information concerning many personality variables beyond an appraisal of intellectual functioning and ego status. One of the important indices is that of affectivity. The incidence of immature and predominantly egocentric affect is proportionately about the same in both groups. On the other hand, the evidence concerning the dominance of mature affect over immature affect is markedly different. Twelve cases, or nearly one third, of the Kibbutz sample show this dominance, whereas only four non-Kibbutz children (less than one eighth of this sample) produce similar results. Moreover, a larger proportion of the non-Kibbutz children's records reflect constriction or avoidance of affective responses altogether.

An over-all impression with regard to affective maturity is that the Kibbutz children hold up well in comparison with their non-Kibbutz counterparts. A greater proportion of them show a relatively high level of emotional maturity and a smaller proportion show immaturity and constriction.

C. Adjustment "signs"

Fifteen of Davidson's (1950) signs of adjustment which are readily evaluated from the Rorschach protocol were also tabulated for both groups. The author defines adjustment as "inner stability and maturity," "degree of rational control in emotional situations" and the degree of rapport with the outside world. In a sense the elements of this definition comprise what would also be called ego maturity and ego strength.

The signs have been empirically arrived at although they are primarily based on Rorschach interpretive hypotheses. A fair sampling of studies with children and adolescents, reported by Davidson (1950), buttresses the construct validity of the adjustment index based on these signs.

Table 6-4 summarizes the differences between the two groups with respect to the signs of adjustment. Clearly, the Kibbutz group fares better than the non-Kibbutz group on this index. The difference is small, but statistically significant. Scores range fairly widely in both groups; there are maladjusted children and well-adjusted children in both groups. The relative incidence of these, however, differs and the difference tends to favor the Kibbutz children.

119

Table 6-4 A comparison of the average number of adjustment signs in the Rorschach records of both groups

	Mean	Range
Kibbutz	7.75	4-13
Non-Kibbutz	6.59	3-11
Difference	1.16	$t = 2.08$ $P < .05$

D. Global ratings of levels of maturity

A final method of dealing with the Rorschach material was through "global evaluation." The Rorschach scoring summaries were evaluated for over-all level of maturity by two judges, in addition to the author. The summaries were coded and all 72 records were shuffled in one pile and given to the judges with the instructions to sort them in the following three categories:

I. *immature* for his age,
II. *adequate maturity*—appropriate for a ten year old,
III. *mature* for his age.

The judges were informed that these records were obtained from children ranging in age from 9 to 11 years. No restrictions were made as to the number of records that may be placed in any one category. The number of cases from the Kibbutz and non-Kibbutz groups placed in the three categories by the three judges are listed in Table 6-5. A brief discussion of these findings follows.

Table 6-5 Global evaluation of personality maturity based on Rorschach summaries

	Judge A			Judge B			Judge C		
	I	II	III	I	II	III	I	II	III
Kibbutz	5	15	18	3	26	9	2	21	15
Non-Kibbutz	10	21	3	8	23	3	8	16	10
Chi square		13.51			5.31			4.75	
P		.002-.001			.10-.05			.10-.05	

In the first place, the vast majority of either group is placed in categories II and III; i.e., most of the children in both groups were judged to be of adequate maturity. Second, all three judges placed a *smaller* proportion of the children from the Kibbutz in the immature category. Third, all three judges placed a *larger* proportion of the Kibbutz children in the "mature for his age" category. Thus, the differences in each instance are in the direction of greater maturity of the Kibbutz children. Highly significant differences between the groups (Kibbutz vs. non-Kibbutz) are obtained from the ratings of judge A. The results of the ratings of judges B and C approach significance.

E. Summary

Four approaches to the analysis of the Rorschach data have been employed. Most of the individual Rorschach variables show similar distributions in the Kibbutz and non-Kibbutz groups of the ten year olds. A few of the variables that are considered to be indices of intellectual development and ego maturity tend to place the Kibbutz children in a more favorable light than their non-Kibbutz counterparts. The other analyses converge in the same direction. They all tend to assess the Kibbutz children as more mature emotionally and socially and, as a group, to enjoy better over-all adjustment.

BLACKY PICTURES

A brief description of the Blacky pictures as a projective device designed to assess psychosexual development following Freudian stages, appeared in Chapter 4. As indicated before, the pictures represent eleven different aspects of psychosexuality. The usual procedure is to obtain a TAT-like story about each picture as well as responses to specific "inquiry" questions—scoring being based on a combination of story, inquiry responses and card selection. Since some of our subjects were not very productive on the spontaneous story, and since we wished to attain a greater degree of objectivity in the scoring on which a comparison of groups was to be based, we confined ourselves primarily to the treatment of the responses to the structured inquiry items.

From our knowledge of child rearing conditions and the opportunities for intrafamilial relationships in the Kibbutz, we made some specific predictions regarding some aspects of psychosexual development. These will be treated first. Subsequently the results of comparisons on many additional items for which predictions have not been made will also be presented in detail. Finally, sex differences, on the Blacky dimensions, in the Kibbutz and non-Kibbutz groups will be explored. The control and experimental groups consisted of 40 subjects each (27 males and 13 females in each group).

A. Testing specific hypotheses

Three of the hypotheses stemming from psychodynamic theory, and discussed in detail in Chapter 3, can most appropriately be tested by means of the Blacky pictures. The first hypothesis states that *Kibbutz-reared children will give evidence of low Oedipal intensity.* Cartoon IV of the Blacky pictures is specifically designed to deal with this dimension.

The cartoon is introduced by stating "Here is Blacky watching Mama and Papa. . . ." According to the manual (Blum, 1950), the following questions are asked of boys:

1. How does Blacky feel about seeing Mama and Papa making love? Why?
2. How often does Blacky feel this way?
3. What will Papa do if he sees Blacky peeking?
4. What will Mama do if she sees Blacky peeking?
5. Which would be better—Mama here and Blacky with Papa . . . or Papa here and Blacky with Mama?

Table 6-6 Responses to questions concerning Cartoon IV (Oedipal intensity) — boys

Questions	1			3		4			5	
	K	NK		K	NK	K	NK		K	NK
Fear — jealousy	10	11	Rejection	19	19	14	15	With Mama	10	17
No concern — positive	17	16	Acceptance	8	8	13	12	Papa or other	17	10
Chi square	N.S.			N.S.		N.S.			3.64	
P (one-tailed test)	—			—		—			< .03	

Answers to these questions were dichotomized and are reported in Table 6-6. Answers to question 2 were omitted, for they are dependent on the answers to question 1 and would be meaningless if reported separately. Of the four chi square values, only the last one (question 5) turned out to be significant. More of the non-Kibbutz boys prefer "Blacky with Mama" rather than "Blacky with Papa." Since the scene is a competitive one, presenting the triangular Oedipal problem, we interpreted the greater frequency of "Blacky with Mama" in the non-Kibbutz children as some evidence for greater Oedipal intensity in this group as compared with children in the Kibbutz setting.

A comparison of the groups of girls does not yield the same trends. The only significant difference is in the perception of mother's rejection for peeking which is more frequent in the Kibbutz group. However, rejection by "papa" is also seen almost as often; consequently, interpretations regarding differences in Oedipal intensity would be a bit far-fetched in this context.

Responses to Cartoon VII (Positive Identification) were used in testing the second hypothesis: *the identification of Kibbutz children will be marked by a greater diffusion of objects.* The cartoon is introduced by stating "Here is Blacky with a toy dog. . . ." The responses to the following questions (Blum, 1950) were dichotomized:

1. Who talks like that to Blacky—Mama or Papa or Tippy?
2. Whom is Blacky most likely to obey—Mama or Papa or Tippy?
3. Who is Blacky acting like here—Mama or Papa or Tippy?
4. Which one would Blacky rather be like—Mama or Papa or Tippy?

(Question 5 was omitted because of the difficulty in achieving an objective classification of responses.)

Table 6-7 Responses to Cartoon VII (positive identification) — boys

Questions	1		2		3		4	
	K	NK	K	NK	K	NK	K	NK
Papa	17	19	15	21	18	15	15	22
Mama and Tippy	10	8	12	6	9	12	12	5
Chi square	N.S.		3.00		N.S.		4.21	
P (one-tailed test)	—		< .045		—		< .02	

Two of the four comparisons that appear in Table 6-7 yield significant differences between the groups. Kibbutz boys are most likely to obey either mother and Tippy, or father; the numbers are close to being evenly divided. However, the overwhelming majority of the non-Kibbutz boys indicate the predominant authority of the father. Again, in response to question 4, the vast majority of the non-Kibbutz respondents would rather be like Papa. This over-whelming identification trend is not so obvious with the Kibbutz group; a sizable proportion would rather be like Mama or Tippy.

It would appear, therefore, that the hypothesis is borne out as far as the boys are concerned; the identification of the Kibbutz boys *is* more diffuse and extends to other members of the family as well as to the father.

No clear-cut differences between the groups of girls were in evidence. Both Kibbutz and non-Kibbutz girls show considerable diffusion of identification, thus yielding no significant differences.

The third hypothesis that could be dealt with by the Blacky pictures is the one concerning sibling rivalry. It was hypothesized that *sibling rivalry among Kibbutz children will not be intense.* Cartoon VIII, which is introduced with the statement "Here is Blacky watching the rest of the family. . . ." is designed to tap the feelings with regard to Tippy who seems to be favored by the parents. The questions to which responses are reported in Table 6-8 are as follows:

1. What does Blacky feel like doing now?
2. Does Blacky think Tippy deserves the praise?

5. If Blacky is angry, who is he most angry at—Mama or Papa or Tippy?

(Questions 3 and 4 in the series cannot be treated meaningfully in group comparisons and were, therefore, omitted.)

Table 6-8 Responses to Cartoon VIII (sibling rivalry) — boys

Questions	1			2			5	
	K	NK		K	NK		K	NK
Aggression-attack	4	10	Yes	4	6	Parent	14	8
Passive-positive	23	17	No	23	21	Tippy	13	19
Chi square	3.48			N.S.			2.76	
P (one-tailed test)	< .035			—			< .05	

Two of the items in the table differentiate between the two groups of boys. More of the non-Kibbutz boys harbor aggressive notions upon seeing Tippy as the parents' favorite. A small minority of both groups think that Tippy "deserves the praise." Finally, anger is directed against Tippy by the great majority of the non-Kibbutz boys, whereas only about half of the Kibbutz boys give their anger a similar direction. It cannot be said that the Kibbutz boys are devoid of feelings of sibling rivalry (most of them don't think Tippy deserves the praise). However, the responses of the non-Kibbutz youngsters more often point in the direction of hostility and aggression as a result of the rivalry. Thus, as far as the boys are concerned, there appears to be a confirmation of the hypothesis stated above.

Data on the girls tend to support a similar trend.

On the basis of the preceding analysis it is possible to state that the hypotheses originally formulated have been confirmed to some extent by the Blacky data. Compared with the non-Kibbutz children, the Kibbutz boys and girls (in two of the instances) tend to show less intense Oedipal involvement, less intense sibling rivalry and greater diffusion in identification.

B. Comparisons on other psychosexual dimensions

Concerning the remaining psychosexual dimensions, assessed by

125

means of the Blacky pictures, we have made no specific predictions. The comparisons between the groups are exploratory—an attempt to tease out whatever differences the data may yield. A summary of the few positive results is presented in the Table 6-9. Only the results that show statistical significance (.05 level) are tabulated; "trends" are omitted.

Table 6-9 Summary of differences between Kibbutz (K) and Non-Kibbutz (NK) children on the remaining psychosexual dimensions

Cartoon	Psychosexual dimensions	Differences between	
		boys	girls
I	Oral eroticism	None	None
II	Oral sadism	None	None
III	Anal sadism	K > NK	None
V	Masturbation guilt	K < NK	None
VI	Castration anxiety	K < NK	–
IX	Guilt feelings	None	None
X - XI	Positive ego ideal	None	None
XI - X	Love object	K < NK	None
		(favoring self)	

Responses to Cartoon I show no significant differences between the Kibbutz and non-Kibbutz children. Both groups tend to think that Blacky is "happy" in the picture (while nursing); mother is perceived as happy by a minority of both groups. There is no evidence of a preponderance of oral-erotic fixations in one group as compared with the other. This finding is interesting in view of the reports of the high incidence of thumbsucking among Kibbutz children (Caplan, 1954). Our present results are inconsistent with an excessive degree of oral activity.

With respect to the second oral dimension (oral sadism) the results are equally noncontributory. The trend is for less aggression to be projected in the Kibbutz boys' responses. However, these are mere trends in results which are short of statistical significance.

Much more obvious are the findings based on responses to Cartoon III (anal sadism). The anal-expulsive behavior of the Kibbutz children (boys and girls), in comparison with their non-Kibbutz peers, is readily reflected on this picture. Nearly half of the Kibbutz boys clearly state that Blacky is doing it (relieving himself) between the parents' "houses" because "he is very angry at his parents." Only two of the non-Kibbutz boys respond in a similar manner. Also, some of the Kibbutz girls give indication of similar reasons and intent for "doing it there," whereas none of the control girls respond in a similar manner.

It is interesting to note that the explanation for "doing it there" offered by the non-Kibbutz children was loss of control—"because Blacky had to go" or "he no longer could hold it in," etc. The Kibbutz children did not give this type of answer at all; clear hostile intent was projected in their responses.

Thus, it may be stated that the Kibbutz group is more clearly anally expulsive; although the non-Kibbutz group is less intensely so, it shows some mixture of anal retentive traits as well. It may also be stated that the hostility to the parents is much closer to the surface (consciousness) in the Kibbutz group than in the controls in whom it is much more repressed and more thoroughly defended against.

Next to be considered are the responses to Cartoon V (masturbation guilt). The answers to the questions give no indication of any awareness of masturbation; "cleaning," "scratching," and similar activities are emphasized.

There are no differences between the groups on the first three questions. However, the last two questions show statistically significant differences with respect to anticipated parental responses, between the Kibbutz and non-Kibbutz boys. A higher proportion of the Kibbutz boys indicate that approval from the parents is expected. The proportion of mother's disapproval is the same in both groups; father's disapproval is expected, however, more often in the non-Kibbutz group.

If we are to infer from the lack of approval, and especially from the disapproval, a "guilty conscience" then somewhat greater masturbation guilt may be attributed to the non-Kibbutz boys. The trend does not seem to hold for the girls; if anything, it is in the opposite direction, especially when it comes to approval from the mother.

127

Cartoon VI which was designed to deal with *castration* anxiety in boys yields some interesting findings. The majority of both groups view Tippy's misfortune (tail being cut off) as punishment for some wrong doing he has committed; however, a smaller (significally) proportion of Kibbutz boys tend to feel so. Thus, these findings are quite consistent with those reported earlier in the chapter, concerning the lesser Oedipal intensity in the Kibbutz boys.

As to *guilt feelings*, little evidence of their importance is projected in the responses of both groups. The overwhelming majority of both groups perseverate in attributing to Blacky feelings of hostility or jealousy, or avoid the issue altogether. Kibbutz children tend to blame their parents more often than the sibling (Tippy), whereas the reverse tends to be true of the non-Kibbutz group.

Cartoon X which shows Blacky dreaming about an adult male dog (Cartoon XI—an adult female dog) is concerned with the assessment of the *positive ego ideal*. One item approaches statistical significance: the vast majority of non-Kibbutz boys indicate that Blacky sees himself in the adult role, while only one half of the Kibbutz boys give similar responses. There seems to be somewhat less of a narcissistic quality about the responses of the Kibbutz boys. The girls show less of a differential trend.

Clear-cut evidence in the direction just indicated also appears in the responses to the last cartoon which refers to the *love object* (Cartoon XI for boys, X for girls). About the same proportion of boys refer to Blacky as "dreaming" about mother or another female dog. However, the real differences appear in the fact that about 50 percent of the non-Kibbutz boys report Blacky dreaming about himself, whereas less than 20 percent of the Kibbutz group respond in a similar vein. This, again, points to the comparatively dominant narcissistic orientation of the non-Kibbutz youngsters.

C. Summary

We shall now attempt to integrate the numerous details presented in the data.

The findings are largely negative in the oral sphere. There are no significant differences between the Kibbutz and non-Kibbutz groups in the areas of oral eroticism and sadism. There seems to be little evidence of strong disturbance along these dimensions in either group.

Surprisingly, more Kibbutz children than non-Kibbutz children tend to give indication of anal sadistic trends directed at the parents. The anality appears to be predominantly of the expulsive type. The non-Kibbutz children give indications of less marked expulsiveness, with hostility toward parents not expressed or, perhaps, more deeply repressed.

Only the results obtained with boys are consonant with the hypothesis that Kibbutz children would show evidence of lower Oedipal intensity. The results with the girls do not confirm this position.

Consonant with the lesser Oedipal intensity in the Kibbutz boys, there is slight evidence in support of lower castration anxiety in this group.

Some evidence of greater frequency of guilt feelings in the non-Kibbutz group was obtained. The trend is consistent for both sexes.

As hypothesized, positive identification is more diffuse in the Kibbutz group. This trend is fairly consistent for boys and girls. The differences between the Kibbutz and non-Kibbutz girls are not marked, for the positive identification of the latter is also more diffuse.

Similarly the ego ideal of Kibbutz boys and girls is more diffuse than that of the non-Kibbutz children; the same-sex parent is less often the ego ideal for the Kibbutz children. Other figures, including Tippy, serve the purpose more often.

It was also hypothesized that sibling rivalry will be less intense in the Kibbutz group. Some support for this position was obtained from the data.

Finally, the love objects are more diffuse in the Kibbutz group. The parent of the opposite sex is more often mentioned by the non-Kibbutz boys. In general, the non-Kibbutz group indicated a more narcissistic orientation in this area.

INCOMPLETE SENTENCES

The sentence completion task administered to the ten year olds consisted of 36 incomplete sentences. Nine areas are dealt with, each by four incomplete sentences: Father, Mother, Family, Friends, Fears, Guilt Feelings, Past, Future, and Abilities. The first three areas are in the *intrafamilial* sphere; the "Friends" sentences reflect chiefly *interpersonal* relationships; and the remaining five areas may be subsumed under the title of *self-concept*.

A. Intrafamilial relationships

The incomplete sentences are listed with numbers that correspond to their ordinal position in the children's form of the test.

Father

1. I think that my father only sometimes . . .
10. If only my father were . . .
19. I wish that my father . . .
28. I think that my father . . .

Mother

8. My mother . . .
17. My mother and I . . .
26. I think that most mothers . . .
35. I like my mother, but . . .

Family

7. Compared with most families, mine . . .
16. My family treats me as if . . .
25. Most families I know . . .
34. When I was a small child, my family . . .

Completions of these stems were placed in two categories—"positive" and "other." To be placed in the positive category, the completions had to indicate fairly obviously a positive attitude to father, mother or the family unit; completions that were indicative of a negative attitude or a noncommittal, nonpositive attitude were placed in the "other" classification. Outright negative responses were extremely rare. Most of the nonpositive responses were factual and nonevaluative, as exemplified by the following completions:

(Father)

Positive	Other
1. gets annoyed with me	goes to Jerusalem
10. be healthy all the time, then I would be very happy	be the owner of a toy store
19. will be like he is now	will be a carpenter
28. a good father	is nervous enough

(Mother)

8. is very lovely and also smart	works in the children's house
17. love each other very much	went to Tel Aviv
26. love their sons	are irritated when the children are not OK
35. and I would like to play with her all my free time	only when she is not angry

(Family)

7. is good, smart and lovely	is particularly large
16. I were a princess	I am still an infant
25. are good families	are in the country
34. loved me very much	still lived in barracks

The response pattern to the Father items is remarkably similar for the two groups of boys; the proportions of positive and "other" responses are very much alike. One statistically significant difference between the groups of girls appears on Father item 1. The non-Kibbutz girls tend to give a larger proportion of responses to the positive category; differences on the remaining items are not significant.

The differences on the Mother items are concentrated entirely in the male groups. Here, on three out of the four items, larger proportions of Kibbutz boys gave the positive completions. These differences approach statistical significance $(P < .10 > .05)$.

None of the Family items seem to elicit clear-cut differences between the groups. Although the larger proportions of positive responses are in the Kibbutz group, the analysis merely points to a trend, for statistical significance was not reached.

Still another analysis of the responses of the groups was attempted. This form of treatment of the data may be termed "global." An attempt was made to evaluate the over-all attitude of each individual in each area on the basis of *all four completions* of the sentences in that area. Three judges categorized the attitudes of each subject to father, mother and family on the basis of the sets of completions in these respective areas. The results of each judge are separately presented in Table 6-10.

Table 6-10 Global evaluations, by three judges, of attitudes in the three areas of intrafamilial relationships

Judges	Father				Mother				Family			
	Males		Females		Males		Females		Males		Females	
	K	NK	K	NK	K	NK	K	NK	K	NK	K	NK
1	*			***	***		0		**		0	
2	0			*	*		0		**		*	
3	0			****	***		0		*		*	

0 No difference between groups

* Positive trend; not significant statistically

** Positive direction: $p = .10$-$.05$

*** Positive direction: $p = .05$-$.02$

**** Positive direction: $p < .01$

Whereas some of the differences previously noted were based on findings with one *individual item* or another, the global treatment seems to strengthen the findings. In the Family area, moreover, individual item comparisons did not yield statistically significant differences, although trends were perceived. Those trends are fortified by the global judgment. Essentially Table 6-10 enumerates differences in positiveness of attitude by indicating, by means of asterisks, the groups in which positive attitudes have been expressed with greater frequency.

We note the marked tendency of the non-Kibbutz girls to show positive attitudes toward the father figure; all three judges point in this direction, and the results of two of them are statistically significant. There are no important differences in this area between the groups of boys.

A reverse position is obtained in the mother area. Here no differences appear between the girls, whereas the Kibbutz boys show greater positiveness in attitude when compared with the control group.

Attitudes in the family area tended to be more frequently positive in the Kibbutz group, as indicated by the responses to individual items. The global judgments are consistent with these trends and lend added weight to them. The greater positiveness (compared with non-Kibbutz individuals) is more marked in the Kibbutz males than in the Kibbutz females; both sexes, however, show the same trend.

B. Interpersonal relationships

Incomplete sentences in the area of Friends are the only ones to be considered here. (Some other areas were included in the adolescent form which will be discussed in the next chapter.) Completions of the following stems will be discussed:

6. In my opinion a good friend should . . .
15. I don't like people who . . .
24. The people I like best . . .
33. When I'm not near them, my friends . . .

Item 6 calls for qualifications of a "good friend." Responses were classified in three categories. When the reference in the completion was to the respondent himself, it was classified as "self-reference" (e.g., "help me with everything"). The category of "help—devotion" was reserved for those responses which do not include self-reference though similar attributes are emphasized (e.g., "help at work and be nice"). Under the category of *personality* all completions that stress some general personality characteristics of a good friend were classified (e.g., "be a good person"). No significant differences between the Kibbutz and non-Kibbutz

133

groups in the distribution of responses were found on any of the items. It is interesting that such differences are not elicited in view of the dissimilar kinds of experiences to which the two groups of children have been exposed.

C. Self-concept

Five areas, or 20 of the 36 items of the children's form, constitute what may be broadly described as the self-concept sphere. The areas are: Future, Goals, Abilities, Fears and Guilt. The first three deal primarily with achievement, self-confidence, hopes and expectations, i.e., more positive aspects of the self. Fears and guilt are the negative side of the coin and imply certain attitudes which are undesirable and inimical to optimal functioning. Each area, however, offers the opportunity for the projection of both positive and negative self-reflective attitudes. We shall deal with each of the areas separately and in the order listed above.

Incomplete sentences in the Future area are as follows:

4. The future appears to me . . .
13. I hope . . .
22. One of these days I . . .
31. When I will be older . . .

In a sense, the first item (4) differs from the others in this group; it is more abstract and requires less specific responses than the other three. Yet, although the majority of both groups responded in a general, and a positive, way to the future ("very beautiful"), quite a few completions departed from the general descriptive trend. Very few subjects viewed the future with doubt and uncertainty ("difficult"). A few of the Kibbutz group and only one of the non-Kibbutz group mentioned broad social or national achievements, such as "that the land of Israel will be blooming and beautiful." Finally, a small proportion in each group dealt with the future in a concretely personal fashion by referring to specific and relatively immediate personal expectations (e.g., "I shall take a trip to Haifa during vacation"). Differences between the groups appear to be minor; a slightly more pessimistic trend and greater concern with broad social-national goals among the Kibbutz children may be noted.

A trend similar to the one just discussed appears in the responses to item 13 in the Future area. Nearly twice the proportion of Kibbutz youngsters "hope" for broad social events such as "in another year there will be peace between Israel and the Arabs," as compared with those of the non-Kibbutz group. However, similar proportions hope for immediate personal events ("I will catch up with the kids in arithmetic") and for more distant personal goals ("that I will be a teacher when I grow up"). No significant differences on item 13 were obtained.

The next two items (22 and 31) elicited responses which were similarly classifiable in two categories—long-range and short-range goals or expectations. "I shall be an agriculturist" is an example of the former, while "I shall go for a swim in the pool" illustrates the latter category. Item 31 elicits significant differences between the two groups. The direction of greater frequency of long-range goals and a more extended future time perspective favors the non-Kibbutz group. A much larger proportion of Kibbutz children (even when completing the stem "When I will be older") respond with statements of expectation of trivial or recreational activities rather than of, what might be termed in our society, more "mature" plans and goals ($P < .002$).

The classification of responses just discussed carries readily over to the Goals area which is very similar to that of the Future as far as the nature of the elicited responses is concerned. Incomplete sentences in the Goals area are as follows:

3. I always wanted to . . .
12. I could be perfectly happy if . . .
21. My secret ambition is . . .
30. My aim in life is . . .

Inspection of Table 6-11 clearly reinforces the tentative impression, with respect to the differences between the groups, gained from the Future items. Immature and short-range goals predominate in the Kibbutz group. The number of omissions for item 21 is reported, because most of them represent a refusal to disclose the "secret ambition." Some of the children said so directly to the examiner—"If my ambition is secret, why should I tell you about it?" Here, a larger proportion of the Kibbutz group prefers to keep the secret.

Although the last item in the table lists four categories, the chi square calculations and the resulting level of confidence are based only on three categories; the "altruistic" category was combined with the "mature and long-range" category. The differences between the groups are highly significant, thus strengthening the trend already observed in previous items. "To invent something for humanity" or "to develop the country" are examples of the altruistic "aim in life." The fourth category (personal attributes) does not contribute to the over-all differences in the distributions. Self-development rather than any external aim or achievement is involved in this category; e.g., "to study," "to live," etc.

Table 6-11 Responses to Goals items

	K	NK		K	NK
Item 3*			Item 12		
Mature & long range	25	19	Mature & long range	25	12
Immature & short range	67	25	Immature & short range	62	32
Item 21**			Item 30***		
Mature & long range	26	23	Mature & long range	27	29
Immature & short range	35	8	Immature & short range	23	1
Omitted	30	12	Altruistic	6	0
			Personal attributes	23	13

*P < .10 > .05   **P < .02 > .01   ***P = .001

Third among the areas constituting the self-concept is Abilities (*see* Table 6-12). Sentences concerned with this area are as follows:

2. When I have no hope to succeed . . .
11. I think I have the capacity to . . .
20. My greatest weakness is . . .
29. When my luck is bad . . .

A rather high proportion of the Kibbutz group reacts with sadness and discouragement to failure (item 2); the reactions are emotional in nature ("I am sad," "I get nervous"). The non-Kibbutz proportion in this category is much smaller. Most of the non-Kibbutz children report a rather neutral and fatalistic reaction ("then I don't succeed"). About the same percentages of subjects in both groups do not accept failure and remain hopeful ("I try again"). The differences on item 2 meet the test of statistical significance.

Table 6-12 Responses to Abilities items

	K	NK		K	NK
Item 2*			Item 29		
Sad-discouraged	47	12	Sad-discouraged	57	30
Hopeful	11	5	Hopeful	—	—
Neutral	30	26	Neutral	15	8
Item 11			Item 20**		
Work & study	41	28	School subjects	36	4
Recreation	29	12	Physical infirmities	26	18
			Undesirable habits	14	11

*P < .02 > .01   **P < .002

Item 11 yielded responses that could be easily dichotomized. Those who believe they "have the capacity to do 'arithmetic'," or "to take care of babies" were placed in the work and study category. Completions such as "stand on my head and hands" or "do a three meter broad jump" were classified as recreation. Although a higher proportion of Kibbutz children may be placed in the latter category, the differences are short of statistical significance.

"Weaknesses" (in response to item 20) were given a threefold classification: those referring to school subjects ("reading," "division," etc.); those referring to physical infirmities ("headaches," "when I get an injection," etc.); and those referring to undesirable habits, such as thumbsucking, nervousness. Here the differences between the two groups are quite significant. Nearly half of the Kibbutz children are concerned with scholastic shortcomings while a negligible proportion of the controls show similar concern. The majority of controls interpret weakness primarily in a physical sense.

Item 29, although similar in content to item 2, does not differentiate between the groups to the same extent. Only two of the response categories of item 2 were represented. No additional illustrations are needed for they would duplicate those already cited.

Earlier, reference has been made to the two "negative" areas in the self-concept sphere—Fears and Guilt. Incomplete sentences covering the Fears are as follows:

5. I know it is silly, but I am afraid . . .
14. Most of my friends don't know that I am afraid . . .
23. If only I could be afraid no more . . .
32. Because of my fears I sometimes have to . . .

The first three items elicit responses with respect to the nature of the fears—the objects that stimulate them. Animals are mentioned by the majority of subjects in both groups: lions, jackals, snakes and even dogs are mentioned quite often. Another category, that of fear of physical hurt (e.g., "injections," "being hit," or "death"), is applicable to items 5 and 23. No significant differences were obtained on these two items.

Item 14, although evoking the usual animal responses, seems to have tapped some other fears in a sizable proportion of both groups; these are entitled "interpersonal" and fears of night and darkness. The interpersonal fears refer to persons rather than animals or situations that are seen as dangerous—"children who throw rocks," "the teachers," "grade 5," etc. A larger proportion of the Kibbutz children mentioned this type of fear as well as fear of the night and darkness. The differences between the groups on this item are significant statistically.

Item 32, the last in this area, is different in nature from the others for it does not yield responses about the kinds of fears but about methods of handling them—about behavior which is caused by them. Here, both groups are quite similar in their reactions. Withdrawal seems to be the most popular method employed in avoiding the source or stimulus of the fear, by both groups. "Run away," "retreat" are responses in this category. Next in frequency are a variety of emotional reactions reported in response to fears—"cry," "be ashamed," etc. A small number of subjects in both groups indicate methods of control and attempts to "overcome" the fears, "call for help," "protect myself," etc.

The remaining sentences of the children's form are in the area of Guilt. The four incomplete sentences are:

9. If only I could forget the moment that I . . .
18. My greatest mistake was . . .
27. When I was younger I felt guilty about . . .
36. The worst thing that I did in my life . . .

Although the sentence stems were designed to evoke memories about forbidden behavior (or intentions) and the consequent guilt feelings, the responses do not fulfill such expectations in every instance. Guilt is by no means the universal response to item 9. A minority of both groups indicates the wish to "forget the moment" when they committed a misdeed of some sort—"did a bad thing," "hit somebody," etc. A majority of both groups reports memories of discomfort, primarily of a physical nature—"was very hungry and thirsty," "get hit," "get a headache." Still others wish "to forget" fear-arousing situations, but not feelings of guilt or pangs of conscience. Responses such as "dream about a lion," "am scared," etc., belong to this category. Apparently fear and discomfort are, at this age level, more central than feelings of guilt or "moral anxiety" (superego anxiety). This observation holds for both groups of children; no significant differences between them were found.

Guilt is more clearly focused in the remaining three incomplete

139

sentences in this area. There is no question whether guilt is in fact experienced, rather the responses are elicited to throw light on the *content* or the *reasons* for guilt feelings. The majority of subjects of both groups regret aggressive behavior. This category includes actual physical aggression—"I hit somebody," "I hit a girl in class" —and psychological aggression—"I insulted a friend after a quarrel," "I annoyed the teacher," or "I angered mother."

The "other" category includes all responses that are classifiable as misbehavior but not directly as aggressive behavior. This category includes sins of commission—"I lied," "I cheated somebody"—and sins of omission—"I didn't come to visit father when he was sick."

All three items (18, 27 and 36) were similarly dichotomized. The results on these items, and in this area in general, emphasize the similarity between the groups rather than dissimilarity. None of the differences between the Kibbutz and non-Kibbutz samples are statistically significant. Apparently, with respect to the contents of the superego, we cannot say that different cultural mores have been internalized by the two groups; they both partake of the same broad ethics of the larger Israeli Judaic tradition.

A brief summary is in order. Of the twenty chi squares, based on comparisons between the groups on the self-concept items, five are statistically significant at the .05 level of confidence or beyond. This is better than chance, for by chance alone only one of these comparisons would have turned out to be significant statistically.

With respect to Goals and Future we note a somewhat paradoxical situation in the Kibbutz group. On the one hand, members of this group tend more often to be concerned with short-range and trivial goals; on the other hand, more subjects of this group cite lofty, selfless and altruistic aspirations indicating concern for the community, the nation and the larger social unit. Perhaps the lack of continuity in role (to which we shall allude later in greater detail) between the Kibbutz child and adult is responsible for the shorter time range in goals and expectations and for the greater concern with shortcomings in the current school situation (item 20 in the Abilities area).

It also appears that the Kibbutz child more often views his failure ("no hope to succeed") with discouragement and negative emotional reaction than accept it philosophically. Although there are no differences on the Guilt items, the previously mentioned discouragement may point to a trend of guilt about failure to achieve or to succeed.

Of interest are also the differences in the area of Fears. Interpersonal relations are more fraught with anxiety for a greater proportion of the Kibbutz youngsters. Perhaps the need for continuous vigilance in their day-by-day living produces special anxieties about interpersonal issues, although a greater facility in group living may be part of the picture. The night and darkness is another fear hardly mentioned by the non-Kibbutz group. One may speculate about residues of possible feelings of isolation experienced at night during Kibbutz children's infancy in the children's house.

INTEGRATION OF FINDINGS

A provisional attempt to integrate the findings of this chapter needs to be made at this juncture. (We shall have to wait for final integration until all of the data have been presented for all the age groups.)

From the mass of data, obtained through the employment of different psychological techniques and methods, we need to extract some major trends and correlate them with each other whenever appropriate, i.e., whenever they refer to similar concepts and constructs. The problem is complicated by the fact that different techniques tend to tap information at different levels of awareness and involve varying degrees of inference vis-a-vis the projective hypothesis.

It may be worthwhile to deal first with the simplest type of measure, which is closest to the usual psychometric devices in its nature and results, the Goodenough test. The results indicate that the Kibbutz children are by no means inferior to the non-Kibbutz children on this measure of intelligence; the trend is in the direction of greater superiority of the Kibbutz group. Such a trend (which approaches statistical significance) is a reversal of the one noted in the infant groups. If we are to assume, and it is a reasonable assumption, that *these* Kibbutz ten year olds as infants would have tested

141

below non-Kibbutz controls on measures of general development, we must note that this relative inferiority is not maintained in later years. They seem to "catch up" with the non-Kibbutz group, nay, even surge ahead of it.

Further evidence in support of the trend of relative superiority of the Kibbutz group is derived from the Rorschach findings. Broader indices, such as "ego strength" and "adjustment" as well as emotional maturity, elicited by means of the Rorschach method, seem to yield results favoring the Kibbutz group. *As a group,* therefore, the Kibbutz children appear to be more mature emotionally, better adjusted, and more developed perceptually—an important aspect of ego development. These findings are quite consistent with the overall relatively high intellectual level derived from the Goodenough test, for the Kibbutz group.

Progression through the psychosexual stages of development and the vicissitudes arising in conjunction with such a progression are of primary importance in the dynamics of personality. The earliest stage, that of orality, seems to yield no important differences between the two groups studied. If anything, there is an oral fixation trend in the non-Kibbutz group rather than among the Kibbutz children. "Oral deprivation" which might be inferred from a high incidence of thumbsucking among the Kibbutz children apparently is not a justified assumption. The Blacky does not support the notion that orality is a major area of difficulty. Anality, on the other hand, of the expulsive variety with sadistic implications, does seem to be an important characteristic of the Kibbutz sample. One may wonder, however, whether the open hostility toward the parents exhibited in this connection is not really directed more at the parent-surrogates, the metaplot who are in charge of toilet training and enforcement of cleanliness. This hypothesis may be further reinforced by the results obtained with the incomplete sentences. Attitudes toward parents are consistently quite positive among Kibbutz children. These attitudes, however, are at a more conscious level; the question of greater defensiveness may therefore be raised in this context.

At least as far as the boys are concerned, Oedipal intensity is not so great for the Kibbutz children. Because of the lower intensity in the relation to, and dependence upon, the biological mother, the rivalry with the father is felt much less intensely. This fact gives rise to less intense and less clear-cut positive identification with the father figure. On the Blacky, identification seems to be a more diffuse state of affairs as far as the Kibbutz youngster is concerned, for the father is not really the agent of the most "decisive frustration" (Fenichel, 1945). The pattern of more diffuse identification is further supported by the findings on the sexual differentiation scale. Here, too, the Kibbutz children are less effective in the role differentiation between masculinity and femininity, thus implying less concern or vigilance with respect to masculine and feminine roles.

Consistent with the trend of lower Oedipal intensity is also the finding with respect to sibling rivalry. The diffusion of attachment to parents and parent surrogates and the additional fact that the Kibbutz child is "born with a group of siblings" with whom he lives throughout his childhood reduce the intensity of sibling rivalry. Hence, the attitudes to the family unit as reflected in the sentence completion findings are also more positive and less fraught with ambivalence for the Kibbutz children.

Although no differences between the groups with respect to the guilt dimension on the sentence completion test were evident, some trends appear on the Blacky. Here, self-blame, less approval on the part of the parents, and guilt about hostile feelings toward the sibling seem to characterize more of the non-Kibbutz children. Yet, with regard to anxiety (as opposed to fear of an objective nature) there is a tendency for the Kibbutz children to report it more frequently, on the sentence completion.

An interesting finding in the comparisons is the greater incidence of narcissistic orientations of the non-Kibbutz youngsters. The dreams attributed to Blacky are usually about the self and much less often about parents, siblings or other figures. This trend is marked in the non-Kibbutz boys, but less clear for the girls. One may, perhaps, note a consistency between the narcissistic orientation of the non-Kibbutz children (especially with respect to the ego ideal) and their aims, goals and future expectancies as projected in their responses to the incomplete sentences. Here they reveal more of an independent sort of long-range planning and future perspective than the Kibbutz children for whom the short-range, immediate type of goal is more characteristic. We shall have more to say about this consistency and some of the other points in subsequent chapters.

GENERAL SUMMARY

1. Intellectually the Kibbutz children are at least as well developed as, and to some extent surpass, the non-Kibbutz children. This finding represents a reversal of the trend noted with the infants, reported in the previous chapter.

2. Evidence concerning ego-strength, emotional and overall maturity and general adjustment favors the Kibbutz children.

3. Some minor trends point to greater anxiety among the Kibbutz children and greater guilt (superego anxiety) among the non-Kibbutz children.

4. Lesser intensity of Oedipal attachment and greater diffusion of the identification process are more characteristic of the Kibbutz sample.

5. Kibbutz children show more positive attitudes toward the family unit and less intense sibling rivalry than their non-Kibbutz peers.

6. There is some evidence of greater hostility of the Kibbutz children toward parental figures at a deeper, unconscious level; at a more conscious level these attitudes of the boys appear more positive to the mother figure and the attitudes of the girls less positive to the father figure than those of the parallel non-Kibbutz groups.

7. Kibbutz children tend to be less narcissistically oriented in their object choices.

8. As far as goals and future expectancies are concerned, the Kibbutz youngsters tend to emphasize either short range and recreational activities or broader altruistic aims as compared with the non-Kibbutz children whose goals are long-range personal expectancies involving more extensive future time perspectives.

Of course, the similarities between these groups of children are probably more numerous than the differences or dissimilarities. However, our general purpose is to relate personality conditions to antecedent and early childhood experiences. For such a purpose our emphasis on differences is a necessary strategy.

7.

Adolescence:
The Seventeen Year Olds

In the previous chapter we noted that the Kibbutz children have made notable advances during the years between infancy and pre-adolescence—advances in intellectual development and personality maturity which placed them in a fairly favorable position when compared with non-Kibbutz children of similar age. The important question that arises is whether such changes are transitory or whether they persist through later years and presage adolescent and adult development and status. Are the gains made by the growing Kibbutz children maintained and consolidated—are they able to hold their own in later years? To answer this question we have studied groups of seniors in the secondary school systems: 30 Kibbutz adolescents and 25 non-Kibbutz adolescents, of both sexes, with an average chronological age of about seventeen and one-half years. They represent several Kibbutzim and several ordinary villages.

Three major methods of assessment were employed, two of them almost identical with the ones used with the children—the Rorschach and the sentence completion test. The latter is a 59 sentence form containing the children's 36 sentence form. Instead of the Blacky several suitable TAT cards were employed, in an attempt to get at some of the intrafamilial and interpersonal dynamics of the adolescents.

145

For a number of reasons, well known to the field worker in a foreign country, not all techniques were administered to the total sample. Some attrition occurred. Consequently, the number of subjects reported will vary somewhat with the technique employed.

Rorschach Results

This test was administered individually to 26 Kibbutz and 22 non-Kibbutz adolescents. The proportion of boys was somewhat larger than that of girls in each group. For purposes of the analysis of results with this method, no breakdown as to sex appears to be necessary. Generally, the analysis of the Rorschach findings will follow the procedure outlined for the ten year olds. Some additional attention to the content of the records will be paid in the present context, for the protocols of the adolescents were longer and more productive.

A. Some variables and indices

A comparison of the two groups of adolescents on a number of significant Rorschach factors that mainly reflect intellective and ego development status was first undertaken. The results reveal some interesting trends.

On three of the variables the differences between the groups approach significance, in favor of the Kibbutz adolescents. A larger proportion of the Kibbutz adolescents show greater productivity, i.e., richness and spontaneity in their psychological functioning. Also, more of the Kibbutz group respond with a larger number of movement responses which are interpreted as indices of inner living, inner control and imaginative capacity. Along with that, the proportion of Kibbutz adolescents producing large numbers of responses indicative of awareness of social norms, i.e., popular responses is also greater. A trend toward an excessive degree of conventionality and conformity may perhaps be inferred from this finding.

On some of the other variables, such as intellectual organization activity and number of content categories, the proportion of the Kibbutz group among the high scorers (above the combined median) is greater, but the results are not statistically significant. No clear-cut or significant trend is discernible in the other variables.

Another finding of interest involves differences in "first response reaction times." With few exceptions, the Kibbutz adolescents respond more quickly in the testing situation. There is a significant difference between the medians for the two groups in the reaction time to the first Rorschach card. In other words, when presented with a novel situation, the Kibbutz adolescents respond with greater speed, security, less anxiety and less inhibition.

The groups are similar as far as structural relationships between affectivity and inner controls are concerned. Although there is a strong trend in what Beck (1960) has termed *experience actual* favoring the Kibbutz adolescents, the differences failed to be supported by the customary statistical tests of significance.

B. Index of adjustment

Again, as for the ten year olds, we employed Davidson's (1950) index of "general adjustment" with the present Rorschach data. The same adaptation, i.e., the use of 15 out of the total of 17 "signs," was made. No significant differences between the Kibbutz and non-Kibbutz adolescents was obtained with this index; the average number of signs is 8.04 and 7.95, for the Kibbutz and non-Kibbutz group respectively.

C. Content categories

Conventional content categories employed in Rorschach scoring are so numerous, and the incidence so varied that comparisons are nigh impossible. However, since the Rorschach movement response is said to reflect fantasied behavior, we followed the idea that some need is expressed in its content. Consequently, a classificatory schema of needs became necessary. In this procedure we were guided by Kaplan's work (1954) in which Murray's need categories were employed. We utilized only eight of these categories, since only a negligible number of responses were classifiable in the categories that were omitted.

Of the eight comparisons made, only the "play" category produced statistically significant differences. More subjects (a larger proportion) of the Kibbutz adolescent group fantasied play in their movement responses than members of the non-Kibbutz group. Although the remaining categories did not yield significant differences, a trend of greater incidence of "aggression" in the themes of the non-Kibbutz group and of "activity" and "orality" in the Kibbutz group may be noted.

D. Summary of Rorschach findings

As far as personality structure, as revealed by the Rorschach, is concerned, the Kibbutz and non-Kibbutz adolescents do not differ very markedly. There is some evidence that points to greater spontaneity, production and freedom and richness of fantasy and expression in the Kibbutz group. Also, the Kibbutz adolescents tend to be more secure and less hesitant and anxious when confronted with a new situation where some "regression in the service of the ego" (Schafer, 1954) is necessary.

No significant differences in the overall adjustment of the groups are reflected in our findings; neither are there any differences in affectivity, its direction or control. A content analysis of the fantasy of the adolescents reveals "play" as a significant feature in the Kibbutz group; such needs as activity and orality also tend to appear more prominently in the Kibbutz adolescent records, whereas aggression is a more dominant theme in the fantasy of the non-Kibbutz adolescents.

TAT STORIES

A method *par excellence* for yielding fantasy content, on the basis of which inferences concerning psychodynamic aspects of personality may be made, is the Thematic Apperception Test. Not all of the original 20 cards were employed (*see* Chapter 4). Cards were selected for their high potential in evoking responses from adolescent subjects and also for their potential in stimulating fantasy and stories that deal with interpersonal and intrafamilial relationships, stories concerning love and marriage and other psychodynamic material that might be useful in an overall personality assessment and evaluation of differences between the groups (Bellak, 1954).

Cards 1, 2, 4, 10, 13MF and 14 were administered to all subjects—male and female. In addition, the males wrote stories about cards 3BM, 8BM and 17BM and the females about cards 3GF, and 18GF. Of the 23 non-Kibbutz subjects 12 were males; of the 25 Kibbutz adolescents 15 were males. However, due to the special circumstances of test administration (*see* Chapter 4), most of the data on the latter group are based on 23 records (13 males), for two of the 25 records were very incomplete and practically useless. Moreover, not all of the total of 48 subjects wrote stories to all pictures presented; consequently the data to be reported on individual cards will be based on different numbers of subjects, fewer than the totals mentioned above.

The TAT material will be analyzed in several ways. In the first place, some formal psychometric type of analyses will be reported; these will deal with implications concerning intellectual functioning and productivity. Secondly, we shall concern ourselves with the thematic content obtained from the stories and its relevance to various psychodynamic formulations about these youngsters in the "Sturm und Drang" period. Finally, an attempt will be made to rate the records for "drive" and "control" on the basis of some recently developed indices of these characteristics reported in the literature (Pine, 1960).

A. Assessment of intelligence and productivity

Since the battery of tests, employed with the adolescents, did not contain a direct measure of intellectual level, we attempted to use the TAT stories as a basis for such an assessment. An Israeli psychologist, a native of the country, was given 46 TAT protocols which were fairly complete (23 protocols of Kibbutz and 23 protocols of non-Kibbutz adolescents) and was asked to evaluate them in terms of the intellectual levels of the writers. On the basis of facility in the use of the language, style, complexity of the stories, etc., he classified the subjects into three broad categories—below average, average and superior intelligence. This rater, of course, was not given any information as to the origin of the subjects—Kibbutz or non-Kibbutz. With the exception of two cases, his categorization agreed with the independent ratings made by the author. The results of his ratings are reported in Table 7-1.

Table 7-1 Estimates of intellectual category based on TAT records

Ratings	N	Low	Average	High
Kibbutz	23	2	11	10
Non-Kibbutz	23	3	15	5

Although the two groups do not differ markedly, the trend favors the Kibbutz group. Twice as many from the Kibbutz sample were classified in the "high" (superior intelligence) category; differences in the other two categories were less marked. Since even a collapsing of the categories would not yield a highly significant chi square, it cannot be said with any degree of certainty that the Kibbutz group is, in fact, superior to the non-Kibbutz group in the intellectual sphere. However, we certainly could not make a statement in the opposite direction. We must conclude that, in the verbal sphere at least, the Kibbutz group is as intelligent as, and probably somewhat superior to, the non-Kibbutz group.

Another index, somewhat related to intelligence, is that of productivity. An approximate word count in stories to five of the cards, on which the available material was fairly complete, was made. The procedure was as follows: The actual number of words in a randomly selected line of a given story was counted. This number was multiplied by the number of lines in that particular story; the product, plus the additional words in the unfinished lines was the final count. After the complete counts were made for each story, the median count was obtained for each group. The data are reported in Table 7-2.

Table 7-2 Productivity (median number of words) on five TAT cards

Cards	1	2	4	13 MF	14
Kibbutz	89	100	78	98	98
Non-Kibbutz	81	70	68	65	51

That the Kibbutz adolescents are quite consistently more productive on the TAT becomes quite evident from even a cursory inspection of the table. On all five cards the medians of the Kibbutz group are higher than those of the controls. Incidentally, the figures for the first three cards are somewhat different than those reported in a previous publication (Rabin, 1961a). In that article the data on males only were reported; the present table includes the figures on the females as well. (The females of both groups were more productive than the males, and the differences between the males only are even greater than those reported above.)

Thus, in terms of verbal fluency and productivity the Kibbutz group's superiority is evident. These findings are quite consistent with a similar trend in the Rorschach findings of Kibbutz children and adolescents. A certain freedom of self-expression, spontaneity and, possibly, lack of defensiveness and rigidity may be some of the implications of these results.

We shall now turn to the more substantive findings projected in the TAT stories.

B. Patterns in fantasy; heroes and major themes

In making comparisons of the content of the TAT stories, i.e., the fantasy material of our adolescent subjects, we attempted to employ some of the categories and scoring procedures reported in normative studies of adults (Rosenzweig, 1949; Eron, 1950). With our small samples these methods were only of limited use. The final classifications of content that evolved were primarily dictated by the nature of the material itself and by some of the more traditional guidelines published in the early TAT literature (Murray, 1943). Considerable emphasis, therefore, is placed upon the characteristics of the "heroes" in the stories as well as of the major themes upon which the plots are founded. We shall present the findings and discuss them card by card. In some instances examples of stories by Kibbutz and non-Kibbutz adolescents will also be presented. Sample stories for cards 1, 2 and 4 were quoted elsewhere (Rabin, 1961a).

Card 1. Murray (1943) describes this picture as follows: *"A young boy (who) is contemplating a violin which rests on a table in front*

151

of him." In addition to this factual "manifest" description of the picture, it may be well to add Henry's (1956) "latent stimulus demands" which are based on the cumulative experience and data obtained with the TAT with the broad "American middle class." According to Henry this card deals ". . . with the general issue of impulse versus control, or the question of the relationship of personal demands to outside cultural agents."

(Murray's descriptions and Henry's latent stimulus demands will be quoted in connection with each card.)

The stories in response to card 1 were analyzed and classified in terms of the dominant characteristic of the hero and in terms of the major themes contained in them. Detailed numerical findings were reported in a previous publication (Rabin, 1961a).

An overwhelming majority of Kibbutz adolescents describe the hero, the central figure of the story, as "a child who has a violin" or as a "pupil." No special talents or ambitions are attributed to him. Most of the non-Kibbutz adolescents see either a talented child or one who has to struggle and is in the process of obtaining a violin, despite economic deprivation, or both. Most of the non-Kibbutz themes involve ambition and high motivation for achievement, whereas the Kibbutz themes involve some ambivalence about practice and rejection of the musical endeavor altogether. They view playing or practicing on the violin as not self-motivated, but as a result of pressure exercised by adults in the environment—parents and teachers.

Card 2. "Country scene: in the foreground is a young woman with books in her hand; in the background a man is working in the fields and an older woman is looking on." The latent stimulus demand of this picture involves the "eliciting feelings toward interpersonal interaction, toward parent-child relations, and toward heterosexual relations"; also, "the contrast between the new and the old . . . girl going off for education as opposed to the farm folk." According to Wittenborn (1949) "it may reveal yearnings for independence, ambition . . . the conflict of the socially mobile student."

We were particularly interested in the relationship between the characters portrayed in the stories and the interpersonal interaction reflected in their themes. First, as to the identification of the characters in the dramas portrayed. More than 90 percent of the non-Kibbutz adolescents see some degree of blood relationships between two or between all three figures in the picture; most often they are seen as members of one and the same family unit. In contrast, 64 percent of the Kibbutz group indicate such a kinship in their stories. The major themes contained in the stories are even more revealing of the differences between the groups.

Nearly two-thirds (64 percent) of the non-Kibbutz stories on card 2 have conflict as their major theme—conflict with parents or internal conflict over leaving the farm and going to the city, over changing occupational status, etc. Less than one-fifth (18 percent) of the Kibbutz adolescents project this type of theme in their stories. They often merely describe the pastoral scene, farm life, etc., and comparatively rarely perceive conflict between the generations, between the "new and the old," farm and city, and so on.

Card 4. "A woman is clutching the shoulders of a man whose face and body are averted as if he were trying to pull away from her." There is also a hazy image of another woman in the background, not mentioned in the standard description given in the TAT manual. "Attitudes toward heterosexual relationship are . . . of course the central issue of importance in this card," according to Henry (1956). "Refusal to see the sexual implications of this picture is particularly indicative of a type of immature psychosexual adjustment common in young men" is an opinion resulting from Wittenborn's (1949) survey.

Differences in the identification of the characters portrayed are not very remarkable when the three categories are considered individually. However, when they are collapsed we may note that 95 percent of the non-Kibbutz stories specify the relationship between the men and the women as "married" or "in love." We find this to a lesser degree in the Kibbutz stories of which 70 percent delineate this relationship but 30 percent mention no close relationship—just a "fellow and a girl."

More salient differences are discerned when we turn our attention to the themes involved. More than half (52 percent) of the non-Kibbutz stories deal with the issue of infidelity as the central theme, a problem area represented to a negligible extent in the Kibbutz stories (10 percent). Instead, half of the Kibbutz stories have aggression as their major theme, and the woman is portrayed as the pacifier who attempts to prevent revenge and aggression. Thirty percent of the Kibbutz stories deal with outright rejection of love and heterosexual relations (usually the male is portrayed as rejecting the advances of the female).

Card 10. "A young woman's head against a man's shoulder." Since this picture involves close physical contact, the latent stimulus demand raises questions as to how close physical contact is handled and what the reaction is to love objects; "it is also reflective either of the subject's view of his spouse or of the intimate emotional (though not generally sexual) relation between his parents."

Kibbutz adolescents—about two-thirds of them—see the pair portrayed in this picture as related—husband and wife, or parent and sibling. Non-Kibbutz adolescents see the pair more often as lovers; this relationship is seen only by one-third of the Kibbutz group. The inference might be made that for the majority of Kibbutz subjects a close physical relationship means some kind of legitimized institutional relationship (such as marriage). Non-Kibbutz adolescents seem to conceive more freely, of such a relationship as occurring outside the bonds of matrimony or blood kinship—between lovers.

Little difference may be seen in the major themes of the stories; reunion, separation and the embrace of lovers are the scenes represented in the stories in almost equal proportions in both groups (see Table 7-3). However, the conditions under which the dramas take place differ to some extent. Circumstances of war and the imminent departure of the husband or lover for the war seem to be characteristic more of the Kibbutz stories. Not shown in the table, but highlighted in a number of the Kibbutz stories, is the theme of duty to the country versus affection for one's spouse. It is not shown, however, as a real conflict, for there is no question that the duty to the country, service in the armed forces or related branches, seems to come first. Both partners, male and female, accept this dictum stoically, albeit often sadly and anxiously. The Kibbutz story that follows illustrates this point well.

Kibbutz (Card 10)

Yaakov and Ruth knew each other, even before the war of liberation, in the training farm. Approximately a year after the training, the training-group received its land and settled in a Kibbutz in the South. Yaakov and Ruth got married and lived a happy life. Yaakov was a saboteur and returned home only once every two weeks or less often. Every time that he would leave for an "action," Ruth knew that he may not return and she would wait anxiously for his return. The night for exploding the bridge arrived, and Yaakov volunteered to place the dynamite charge. A day before the action Yaakov came home. In the evening he had to part from Ruth; the chances of his escaping from this action were slim. Yaakov knew how strong her love was for him, but there was no one qualified who was available for the action, and he was home at the time, the only one who was not in action. Yaakov knew that many saboteurs like himself have wives and children at home and they go to dangerous assignments, knowing full well what is ahead of them. But, war is always a cruel thing; such is the world. Therefore, it is necessary to say good-bye to Ruth without her knowing whether this is the last goodbye she will hear from him. He got up and stood near the door. Ruth looked at him, into his eyes, and understood what was ahead of him; she rose and fell into his arms.

The following day Ruth heard an announcement on the radio that the bombing of the bridge was successful. It was a daring assignment of one saboteur who was blown up with the bridge.

Non-Kibbutz (Card 10)

The girl saw her future in a small green house, and in it a loving husband and lovely children. For many years did she have this dream, but she did not meet the man who would be able to fill the role of the loving husband. Every night before going to bed she would pray for the fellow. And now, finally she met him. They loved each other very much, and as they were in each other's arms they closed their eyes and saw their future. The future of a young, lone family in the heart of green nature, by a bluish lake.

A sense of frontier pioneering and of strong dedication to a cause, without detracting from the intense love relationship, is depicted in the first story. The second story, one of love and yearning, is much more personal, and perhaps, conventional in terms of Western standards. Both stories were written by girls.

Card 13 MF. "A young man is standing with downcast head buried in his arm. Behind him is the figure of a woman lying in bed." Sexuality is, of course, the important aspect of the latent stimulus demand. "Generally, it suggests subject's attitude toward sex partner and particularly toward the reactions prior or subsequent to intercourse. Relations between sexual and aggressive feelings are often portrayed."

Table 7-3 Characters and major themes in stories of males and females combined (percentages of groups)

Heroes	K	NK	Theme	K	NK		K	NK
Card 10						Conditions		
Married couple	44	20	Reunion	33	30	War	44	25
Lovers	33	60	Eve of separation	33	20	Peace	56	60
Parent & child	22	20	Lovers' embrace	33	35	Other — unclear		15
& other			Other		15			
Card 13 MF						Sex in theme		
Husband & wife	31	30	Murder — rape	6	50	Included	43	70
Lovers	31	30	Illness — death	38	15	Excluded	57	30
Man & woman	19	30	Intercourse	25	15			
Man & prostitute	12	5	Rejection of sex	12	5			
Brother & sister	6	—	Miscellaneous	19	15			
Doctor & patient	—	5						
Card 14						Outcome		
Lad-man	60	64	Based in present	35	45	Positive	65	59
Incarcerated person	40	27	Future oriented	65	55	Negative	10	14
Other (Not clear)	—	9				Uncertain	25	27

Inspection of the first column of Table 7-3 tends to indicate insignificant differences. The main protagonists in the dramas are husbands and wives, lovers, or just men and women. In a few cases, all sexual relationships are obviated by considering the male and female as brother and sister or doctor and patient. However, looking at the theme, at the core of the drama which unfolds, we note some interesting dissimilarities between the Kibbutz and non-Kibbutz adolescents.

In 50 percent of the non-Kibbutz stories aggression (murder) or aggression of an extreme nature, coupled with sexuality (rape), are the major themes; this trend is almost completely absent from the Kibbutz adolescents' stories. Instead, death and illness of the woman and the concern of the male are the themes frequently represented in their stories. Sexual intercourse, accompanied by guilt and rejection of sexuality are also fairly frequent themes in Kibbutz stories. Most of the Kibbutz stories deal with death and illness as the central themes, avoiding sexuality altogether, whereas even the murder stories of the non-Kibbutz group have varying degrees of the sexual component. A further look, at the third column of the table, yields more information regarding the overall sexual dimension. In more than half of the Kibbutz stories sexuality is excluded altogether, no allusions being made to it in the relationship between the male and the female. This is true of about a third of the non-Kibbutz stories. Kibbutz stories deal with illness or death of a "friend," a doctor trying to help his patient, and a brother visiting his injured sister.

Two contrasting stories are presented below:

Kibbutz (Card 13 MF)

A pair of youths got acquainted in school and fell in love. They built it up, became a young couple, and in time decided to get married. But the fellow decided that they were still young and that there is still time. Once, when they were in the girl's room, alone, the girl decided to attract him to the deed. She undressed and laid in bed in order to tease him and tempt him. But, the young man who was of a strong character and mind, turned away from her and did not yield. The girl who was very much offended by this, got up and got dressed and chased the young man away from her, forever. Thus ended the romance.

Non-Kibbutz (Card 13 MF)

A couple lived in peace and happiness. But, with the economic crisis the husband became impoverished and therefore began drinking. Once when he came home he was possessed by a murderous anger which comes as a result of drunkenness, he attacked his wife and choked her. After he sobered up he saw what he had done.

In the picture we see a dead girl lying in bed and her husband standing by the bed and crying.

In the morning the police will come and arrest the fellow for the murder of his wife.

Both of these stories were written by boys. The Kibbutz story, although a story of young love, portrays the girl as a temptress and the boy of "strong character" who is able to withstand temptation. However, it is not a rejection of sexuality altogether; it is a postponement, in keeping with the strong taboos and prohibition of the youth movement and of the "youth society." Along with this, there is a realization of the consequences of the rejection of sex for the romance. The story places self-control and strength of character above immediate needs and desires; it is postponement rather than complete negation of sex that is emphasized.

Problems more prevalent in the broader society, "outside" the Kibbutz are interwoven in the non-Kibbutz story. Economic conditions and alcoholism bring a fit of rage and subsequent murder. Some links are missing as to the causes of the underlying murderous impulses; but the ambivalence in the husband-wife relationship, the combination of love and aggression, are probably there more than in the Kibbutz stories.

Card 14. *"The silhouette of a man (or woman) against a bright window. The rest of the picture is totally black."* This card was among the least productive as far as significant thematic material is concerned, although the latent stimulus demand refers to "self-ambition, fantasy and daydreaming . . . degree of ambition and organization of the subject's future planning." Very little material of a daydreaming nature or dealing with future planning was actually produced by either group of subjects. Although the percentage of future-oriented stories given by the Kibbutz sample is somewhat higher, the differences of ten percent is not remarkable. No noteworthy differences are forthcoming from a comparison of the outcome of the stories; the proportion of positive, or bright, and negative outcomes is about the same for both groups.

Thus far the discussion revolved about the data reported on six TAT cards which were administered to both sexes (1, 2, 4, 10, 13 MF and 14). In addition, some cards administered exclusively to males (3BM, 8BM and 17BM) and some exclusively to females (3GF and 18GF) are also to be considered.

Card 3 BM. "On the floor against a couch is the huddled form of a boy with his head bowed on his right arm. Beside him on the floor is a revolver." The latent stimulus demand involves "associations of loss, guilt, attack, and aggression . . . attitudes to the isolated self tend to be aroused."

In the first place, it is interesting to note that more than half of the boys in either group identify the figure as female rather than male. It may reflect, perhaps, a certain cultural bias, namely, that dejection of the kind portrayed in the picture is more characteristic of the female. Again, as noted in stories to card 13 MF, aggression-murder form the central theme of the antecedent conditions for a sizable percentage of non-Kibbutz subjects and a negligible percentage of Kibbutz subjects. Dejection because of failure to achieve or to meet standards is present in several Kibbutz stories, but entirely absent in the non-Kibbutz ones. Depression consisting of crying and contemplation of suicide accounts for 50 percent of the Kibbutz stories' consequences. Depression accounts for only 25 percent in the non-Kibbutz stories, and contemplation of suicide is not mentioned in them. Because of the relatively high proportion of murders in the non-Kibbutz stories, consequences of "regret and atonement" are also more frequent. It is interesting to note that half of the Kibbutz subjects referred to the weapon (revolver, knife) specifically; none of the other group made such a reference although from the content of their stories the awareness of the weapon may be implied. Perhaps specific mention of the weapon was too threatening to the non-Kibbutz boys who gave fairly aggressive stories anyway.

Card 8 BM. "An adolescent boy looks straight out of the picture. The barrel of a rifle is visible at one side, and in the background is the dim scene of a surgical operation, like a reverse image." According to Henry, this picture is "a stimulus test of the subject's reality orientation as well as of his ambition and future planning skills." Also—"it permits hostile and attacking fantasies to emerge."

Table 7-4 Characters, major themes and outcomes in TAT stories: males (percentages of groups)

	K	NK		K	NK		K	NK
Card 3 BM								
Hero			Theme			Consequence		
Male	25	42	Murder	8	33	Crying — unhappy	17	25
Female	75	58	Abandonment	42	42	Regret — atonement	8	25
			Future	25	–	Contemplation of		
			Other	25	25	suicide	33	–
						Lonely	25	25
						Miscellaneous	17	25
Card 8 BM								
Hero (operated on)						Outcome		
Father	46	42	War — revolution	46	17	Positive — recovery	23	33
Self	8	17	Boy shot father	–	17	Negative — death	23	8
"Man"	38	33	Injury — illness	46	50	No outcome	16	42
Not specified	8	8	Other	8	17	Ambition — future	38	17
Card 17 BM								
Theme			Direction					
Escape	36	75	Ascending	64	41	Positive	28	42
Performance	14	8	Descending	21	25	Negative	50	33
Sport — training	50	16	Uncertain	16	33	Uncertain	21	25

No great dissimilarities in the identification of the figure on the operating table and, by implication, of the relationship of the boy in the foreground to that figure, are evident in the figures presented in the first column of Table 7-4. However, the next two columns of this Table point to some interesting and, perhaps, meaningful differences in the stories told to card 8 BM. Nearly half of the Kibbutz boys see the condition of the patient in the operating room as a result of some mass struggle—war or revolution. Not so the control group; comparatively few of their stories present such a background. On the other hand, accidental shooting of the father by the boy appears in some non-Kibbutz stories, but is entirely absent in those written by the Kibbutz boys. The remaining categories show no differences.

Story outcomes (third column) differ to some extent for the two groups. Kibbutz boys tend to be less optimistic; they have fewer positive, i.e., recovering outcomes, and more negative ones, involving the death of the hero. On the other hand, Kibbutz stories are more often terminated with plans for the future which emanate directly from some of the tragic outcomes. Finally—a larger proportion of the non-Kibbutz boys offer no outcome; they, perhaps, have more difficulty in dealing with the aggressive stimulus to bring the story to some conclusion.

Card 17 BM. "*A naked man is clinging to a rope. He is in the act of climbing up or down.*" The "subject's concept of the relation of the individual to his environment . . . narcissistic exhibitionism and competitive ideas . . . notions of fear and escape" are some of the latent stimulus demand aspects of this card.

Turning again to Table 7-4, some dissimilarities between the groups can be readily discerned. Perhaps most clearly demonstrated are differences in the themes. Seventy-five percent of the non-Kibbutz boys tell stories of escape; criminals, prisoners and others escape undesirable situations. A much smaller percentage of Kibbutz boys highlight this theme. In contradistinction, a sizable proportion of Kibbutz boys create a recreational setting; the figure in the picture is either a circus performer or is training or competing in a sports event. Most likely, these differences in type of theme are to some degree responsible for some of the smaller differences in the direction of the movement of the figure clutching the rope. As to outcome, the trend demonstrated for card 8 BM is repeated in the present one as well. Kibbutz boys again appear to be less optimistic and more pessimistic—fewer positive and more negative outcomes are summarized in the last column of the findings on this card.

Card 3 GF. "A young woman is standing with downcast head, her face covered with her right hand. Her left is stretched forward against a wooden door." This card is very similar to card 3 BM as far as the latent stimulus demand is concerned; it arouses associations related to pain and depression and the possible reasons for it. Also, the nature of the defenses may be inferred from the stories.

Nearly all of the Kibbutz girls saw the source of negative emotion, portrayed in the picture, as abandonment or rejection by lover or husband. Non-Kibbutz stories are more varied, including prostitution as a possible cause of dejection which is absent entirely in the stories of Kibbutz girls. Most of the results of these antecedent conditions may be categorized as passive attitudes. The majority of both groups do not present an active and assertive outcome beyond the state of depression and unhappiness.

Card 18 GF. "A woman has her hands squeezed around the throat of another woman whom she appears to be pushing across the banister of a stairway." The nature of this card marks it a stimulus of aggression, but "turning it into the opposite" may also be included as a part of its latent stimulus demand. In other words, we are dealing with a stimulus of aggression and/or with modes of covering it up.

Some differential trends between the groups are worthy of notice. First, the majority of Kibbutz girls tend to see the scene as interaction between two women, whereas the non-Kibbutz majority sees a woman-man combination. Secondly, the theme of aggression tends to dominate the Kibbutz girls' stories; non-Kibbutz stories are evenly divided between support (covering up or reaction formation?) and aggression. Apparently more direct expression of aggression in fantasy, and less defensiveness about it, seems to characterize the productions of the Kibbutz female subjects.

C. Summary

A general summary of the qualitative, as well as of the more formal aspects, of the TAT will be presented.

The first issue to be examined is the expression of impulse in fantasy-sexuality and aggression. The themes in cards 4, 10, and 13 MF are particularly relevant. Themes of infidelity (card 4) and of murder and rape (card 13 MF) tend to dominate many stories of the non-Kibbutz adolescents. Thus, considerable heterosexual conflict and sex coupled with aggression appear to be characteristic of this group. "Sexual struggle" in this sense is relatively inconspicuous in the Kibbutz group; instead, the stories tend to project evidences of rejection and, perhaps, repression or suppression of sexuality. Avoidance of the sexual theme or outright rejection of sexuality on card 13 MF, rejection of love on card 4, and the greater proportion of overall exclusion of sexuality in the stories to card 13 MF is some of the evidence that can be marshalled in support of this proposition. Perhaps the greater institutionalization of the close physical relationship in card 10, by seeing more frequently "husband and wife" rather than just lovers, and the placement of the scene on an "emergency basis" (war) is a further indication of a gingerly approach to the issue of close physical relation, especially premarital, among the Kibbutz adolescents.

As far as aggression is concerned, some interesting group differences may be discerned. Aggression is attributed to the heroes more by the non-Kibbutz adolescents than by the Kibbutz group. The differences in the themes on cards 13 MF, 3 BM and 8 BM tend to support this proposition. More of the non-Kibbutz group present the murder-rape theme (13 MF), murder (3 BM) and "boy shooting father accidentally" on 8 BM. Kibbutz adolescents view aggression more in terms of environmental "press," or being aggressed against. Thus, on card 8 BM the stories involving injury are due to war or revolution; card 10 shows a greater emphasis upon war conditions; and card 13 MF stories more often show the hero facing death and illness of his beloved. In the themes to card 4 *intended* aggression is prominent, but its prevention and control are successful in most instances. The only possible exceptions to this general trend are the results to card 18 GF; in these stories Kibbutz girls project more aggression than those of the parallel group.

Secondly, we shall attempt to summarize some of the trends with respect to intrafamilial relationships. Cards 2, 4 and 10 are particularly relevant. Intrafamilial kinship (card 2) is less highlighted by the Kibbutz adolescent; likewise there is less struggle between the "generations." A trend in the same direction may be noted in card 2 in which "husband and wife" are identified less frequently; also, intrafamilial struggle resulting from infidelity is rarely considered. Yet, card 10 elicits stories of tenderness in the relationship between partners, accompanied, however, by sacrifice of the relationship for a higher ideal, such as the defense of the nation. It may also be speculated, in relation to card 8 BM, that the Oedipal intensity is not so great in the Kibbutz group (boys); no accidental shooting of father by the boy occurs in their stories. Thus, whatever relevant material concerning intrafamilial relationships is available, it tends to point to less concern with members of the family in fantasy and to less struggle and ambivalence in the interaction between members of the family.

A few miscellaneous trends may also deserve some comment. Kibbutz adolescent boys tend to give more pessimistic outcomes to their stories than non-Kibbutz boys (cards 8 BM, 17 BM), yet a trend toward greater future orientation in some Kibbutz stories may also be noted (cards 8 BM, 14 and 18 BM). This apparent inconsistency may be summarized as a *concern* for the impersonal and collective future, accompanied by little optimism about it.

D. Drive control

Although the major purpose for the inclusion of the TAT in our study was its usefulness in the substantive analysis of fantasy, another, more formal treatment of the material, was added which concerns itself with "drive control"—an index derived from Pine's (1960) scoring system for the TAT.

Briefly, the scoring procedure is as follows: each story is analyzed for expression of drive content (instinctual behavior or fantasy)—aggressive, libidinal or partial drives. Explicit statements of drive expression are scored; implications and symbolic content are not scored. The scoring system provides a threefold classification of drive content levels. *Level I* is the "direct-unsocialized" drive content "where libidinal or aggressive impulses are directly expressed in a way contrary to conventional social values" (e.g., murder, rape, homosexuality, etc.). *Level II* refers to "direct-socialized" drive as reflected in the content of the story; anger without physical violence, sexual rivalries, and kissing are some examples of content classifiable in this category. *Level III* involves drive content which is "indirect-disguised." Here the drive is inferred and the "underlying impulse is neither explicitly thought nor acted upon in the story." Accidents, death, police are some of the contents from which inferences of drive at this level may be made.

Thus we may note that level I refers to content involving naked impulse expression, whereas levels II and III involve varying degrees of impulse control. The author of this scoring system suggests that "the relationships among the three levels have implications regarding the nature of control operations."

Several of the TAT cards were scored for the levels of drive content. However, in a number of instances several stories had no scorable drive content—an event not readily interpretable in this system. Consequently we selected two cards which were particularly productive, i.e., all of the stories to these two cards yielded some drive content scores. By simply counting the number of level I scores (direct-unsocialized) and the total of level II and III scores (socialized or disguised) in each story, we were able to determine the dominance of impulse or the dominance of control, depending on whichever number was greater.

Table 7-5 A comparison for "drive control" on two TAT cards (number of stories)

Dominant level	Card 4		Card 13 MF	
	K	NK	K	NK
Level I (direct-unsocialized)	0	7	2	10
Level II (direct-socialized) and Level III (indirect-disguised)	12	5	14	10
P (Fisher test)	< .005		< .03	

Results for the two cards are given in Table 7-5. For card 4, the results report a comparison of males only; for card 13 MF, the stories were of males and females combined. The differences between the groups are fairly striking and consistent. On card 4, the Kibbutz subjects did not produce any level I dominant stories; all of the stories were level II and III dominant, indicating drive control. A majority of the non-Kibbutz adolescents fell in the level I dominant category. Similar results were obtained following an analysis of stories told to card 13 MF. For both cards, differences between the groups are statistically significant.

It would appear, from this limited amount of evidence, that the Kibbutz adolescents project in their fantasy a greater degree of socialized and disguised drive content than the controls who more frequently exhibit unsocialized and uncontrolled drive content. It might be pointed out that in most instances the Kibbutz scores were dominated by level II rather than level III content. Generally, the conclusion follows that as far as fantasy dynamics are concerned, most Kibbutz adolescents project control of impulses, whereas fantasy of their control peers more often involves direct impulse expression. How such differences are related to actual *behavior* is another story with which we shall not deal at this juncture.

Before concluding this section, it may be useful to refer briefly to Pine's (1960) description of subjects who use the "modulated" (control) and "unmodulated" (impulse) expression, based on the relationship between the levels and statements of a Q-sort. Subjects who exhibit control or modulation of the expressed drive have "a relatively free intellectual and esthetic expressive style, a flexible identity, non-competitive peer relationships and adequate control over impulses." Also, such subjects tend to have "a capacity to experience and work through conflicts internally."

On the other hand, the level I subjects who use unmodulated drive expression show a tendency toward impulse discharge. Some of the more specific characteristics are: "competitive social relationships, loose thinking, a fear of loss of control, and the absence of a tendency to discharge impulses in internalized ways, such as fantasy."

INCOMPLETE SENTENCES

In addition to the nine areas (Father, Mother, Family, Friends, Goals, Abilities, Future, Fears and Guilt feelings) covered by the 36 item series of incomplete sentences administered to the pre-adolescent group, the areas of Past, Heterosexual Relationships, Superiors, and Colleagues at work and at school, were included in the incomplete sentences form administered to the adolescents. Since one unsuitable item was omitted from the "Superiors" area of the original test ("When I see the boss coming"), the final adolescent form consisted of a total of 59 items. The thirteen areas represented by these incomplete sentences are classifiable in the same general categories as those of the shorter form used with the ten year olds, with one addition—that of sex. Thus, we shall deal with attitudes toward parents and family, interpersonal relationships, self-concept and sex.

A. Attitudes to parents and family

Twelve sentences, i.e., three areas (Father, Mother and Family) are relevant to this intrafamilial dimension. Responses to these sentences were classified in a manner similar to the one described for the pre-adolescents (i.e., positive vs. other). None of the comparisons between the groups yielded statistically significant differences. Generally, Kibbutz and non-Kibbutz adolescents tended to give more positive responses in these areas than did the ten year olds. Most likely, a semi-projective technique such as the incomplete sentences allows for more defensive and socially "appropriate" answers on the part of older subjects who tend to be less frank and direct than younger children. Responses of the adolescents reflect more readily the social norms or "social acquiescence."

A global evaluation resulting from pooling the ratings of two raters yielded similar results—no differences between the groups. The ratings, as described in the previous chapter, were based on all four responses to sentences in a particular area for each subject. No preponderance of positive or other (neutral or negative) attitudes in any one group may be noted. About equal proportions of each

167

group were rated as exhibiting positive (and other) attitudes to father, mother and family. Neither were marked sex differences noted in the results.

B. Interpersonal relationships

Three areas can most appropriately be placed under the rubric of interpersonal relationships—Friends, Work, and Superiors. Since only three stems in the area of Superiors were employed, the results are based on responses to a total of 11 incomplete sentences.

What a "good friend should" do or be (item 7) is conceived of differently by the two groups. Non-Kibbutz youngsters emphasize the readiness of the friend to be of support in emergency situations (e.g., "help me in times of trouble"). This is a relatively minor emphasis in the Kibbutz group which tends to stress more qualities of character and understanding (e.g., "be sincere and wanting to help"). "Help" is stressed by both groups, but the "time of trouble" is omitted in most responses of the Kibbutz adolescents. Apparently the Kibbutz subjects expect help and cooperation at all times, whereas the non-Kibbutz ones are particularly concerned with friendship in states of crisis.

People are disliked (item 20) for their lack of moral stamina and for their shortcomings in interpersonal relationships by the majority of both groups. "Hypocrites, empty and gossipy" people or those who "are not truthful" belong to this category. Kibbutz adolescents tend to show less concern with snobbishness and selfishness as a damning characteristic than do the controls. The egalitarian principles of the Kibbutz society and ideology and the continuous emphasis on cooperation in communal living may be responsible for this difference in outlook.

Responses to item 33 ("The people I like best") present us with what may appear, on the surface, as a paradoxical situation. Here the Kibbutz youngsters tend to emphasize an egocentric orientation; the people they "like best" are those who "treat *me* with sincerity" or "are near to *me*." Non-Kibbutz responses are predominantly not so egocentric but emphasize personality characteristics in a more impersonal fashion; the people they "like best" are those who "treat others nicely," "are honest," etc. There is somewhat greater abstraction in this type of response and greater dissociation from the strictly personal and egocentric orientation. It is interesting to note that several Kibbutz adolescents also mentioned their parents in this connection—an event absent in the responses of the controls. Differences on items 7, 20 and 33 are statistically significant ($P < .05$).

"When I am not near them, my friends . . ." is the last stem (item 46) in the Friends area. A relatively small proportion of both groups exhibits some suspicion ("they talk about me"), but no significant differences were obtained. Several Kibbutz respondents, however, stated that the friends "treat me as if I am among them" or "continue as if I am with them."

Comparison of response categories for the two groups in the Work area yielded two items on which the differences were statistically significant. The results on item 11 ("At work I get along best") clearly reflect the realistic differences in the work conditions of the two groups. Here the Kibbutz youngsters emphasize no special characteristics ("with the rest of the workers") whereas the vast majority of the village boys who work in the private economy of the family mention relatives and friends (e.g., "my parents," "my small brother," etc.). Perhaps, since the Kibbutz adolescent's work experience in the economy at large (as contrasted with that of the youth society and of the "institute") is rather limited, no specific preferences have yet evolved; also, the responses of the non-Kibbutz group reflect the limited range of experience usually confined to the family farming enterprise.

Closely associated with the item just discussed is item 24 in the Work area which involves a characterization of co-workers ("Those with whom I work. . . ."). Here the egocentric orientation is more reflected in the control group, the majority of whom feel that they are appreciated by their co-workers ("are satisfied with me," "understand me well," etc.). The Kibbutz adolescents tend to show more impersonal attitudes and more frequently describe the co-workers in positive terms ("are good workers"), but show less personal involvement. The work situation has perhaps less personal significance for them than it does for the control group. This trend is somewhat reversed on the remaining two items in the Work area, but the differences are not statistically significant.

Only the first item in the Superiors area (item 5: "My leaders. . . .") tends to yield findings indicating differences which approach significance. More Kibbutz adolescents project positive attitudes toward their leaders ("are always right"; "do great work," etc.). Controls tend to be more frequently ambivalent ("were good and bad") or deny having leaders altogether ("are my senses and my intelligence"). The difference in the first item is reflected as a trend in responses to the remaining two stems (items 18 and 44). Teachers, youth group leaders, and other extrafamilial figures are more important and, apparently, are more positively related to in the life of the Kibbutz adolescent.

C. Areas involving the self-concept

The six areas for which the results are presented in Table 7-6 are as follows: Fear, Guilt, Goals, Abilities, Past and Future. With respect to the first two areas in this group, it must be pointed out that large numbers in both groups of subjects either did not respond or were evasive. Apparently admissions of fear and guilt in such a direct fashion is difficult for many adolescent individuals, regardless of origin. The threat of the sentence completion task is clearly demonstrated by the responses to item 6 ("I know it is silly, but I am afraid . . ."). About one-half of the subjects of both groups are "afraid of this" or "of this test."

Fear of death and darkness is admitted to by nearly half of the non-Kibbutz respondents; Kibbutz adolescents mention this infrequently, but concentrate on animals, war and a miscellany of dangers. Several of the latter group state that they are afraid of "nothing" (item 19). This evasive trend is also maintained on item 32.

Although the differences between the groups on item 45 in the Fears area have not been tested statistically because of the small numbers in each cell, the trends are suggestive and interesting nevertheless. They refer to modes of dealing with fears—with defensive operations ("Because of my fears I sometimes have to . . .").

Two predominant methods of dealing with fears characterize most Kibbutz adolescents' responses. First comes the defensive type of operation such as repression, denial, or reaction formation (e.g.,— "not think about them" or "laugh"); second is an active and/or instrumental approach in dealing with fears ("turn on the light at night" or "think about my situation"). On the other hand, the control subjects emphasize more withdrawal from the frightening situation ("give up my plans") and especially the seeking of support and assistance from another person ("go to the doctor" or "be helped by more experienced people"). In the latter situation there seems to be more evidence of dependence. Generally it would appear that the Kibbutz adolescent, when not repressing or denying fears, tends to attack them more actively than the non-Kibbutz controls who respond with withdrawal and reliance on outside help.

All four incomplete sentences in the Guilt area elicit responses which tend to differentiate the groups fairly well. Item 13 ("If only I could forget the moment I. . . .") leaves the choice of a true guilt response or some other kind of completion open to the respondent. Nearly half of the Kibbutz respondents did not project guilt, but a memory of some kind of a physical discomfort, to themselves or to others, for which they are not responsible. Kibbutz adolescents wish to "forget the moment I was hurt" or "I was near a man who was killed." Non-Kibbutz adolescents respond more often with genuine regret for actions of an interpersonal nature. They wish "to forget the moment I lied to my friend" or "hit my sister," etc. Both groups offer approximately equal proportions of the "other" category responses which include completions related to failure in school (non-Kibbutz), fear of termination of school (Kibbutz), and other fears rather than actual guilt.

Item 26 ("My greatest mistake was . . .") elicits a relatively large number of responses related to school from the non-Kibbutz subjects ("that I didn't study well," "to study algebra," etc.); few Kibbutz adolescents respond in a similar fashion; about half of this group resorted to evasion of one sort or another. Perhaps Kibbutz adolescents repress more and therefore do not remember their "greatest mistake." In fact, one Kibbutz adolescent responded with "I don't remember any more" and another, "in my dream."

171

Table 7-6 Areas constituting the self-concept

	K	NK		K	NK
Area: Fears					
Item 6			Item 19		
Present task	13	11	Death — darkness	2	10
Danger: physical	5	9	Other	13	12
Danger: social	3	2			
P	N.S.			< .06	
Item 32			Item 45		
Physical	5	4	Defensive	10	4
Animals	4	—	Withdrawal	2	5
Interpersonal	4	5	Think — act	8	1
Exams	—	5	Seek help	2	7
Evasive	9	5			
Area: Guilt					
Item 13			Item 26		
Physical hurt	7	2	Studies	3	12
Interpersonal	2	8	Moral — interpersonal	8	7
Other	8	8			
P	< .06			< .07	
Item 39			Item 52		
Evasive — denial	12	3	Evasive	13	2
Interpersonal	7	16	Interpersonal	9	12
P	< .01			< .02	
Area: Goals					
Item 3			Item 16		
Culture	13	2	Studies	14	3
Vocation	3	8	Other	10	12
Other	12	15			
P	< .01			< .02	
Item 29			Item 42		
Personal ambition	7	14	Social goals	4	1
Other	18	9	Personal happiness	14	18
			Ambition	7	5
P	< .02			N.S.	

Table 7-6 continued

	K	NK		K	NK
Area: Abilities					
Item 2			Item 15		
Try again	8	8	Vague	9	5
Resign	7	11	Study-work	11	9
			Long-range	4	6
Item 28			Item 41		
Personal trait	17	15	Unhappiness	12	10
Studies	5	1	Change	5	4
"for" something	1	5	Accept fact	10	9
			No significant differences		
Area: Past					
Item 8			Item 21		
Activity & play	15	13	Past State	19	22
Self description	13	10	Future reference	8	2
P	N.S.			< .06	
Item 34			Item 47		
Positive	7	2	Evasive	8	3
Negative	3	–	Family-Social	9	14
Att. Change	6	8	Pers. experience	10	5
Neutral	12	13	P	< .10	
Area: Future					
Item 4			Item 17		
Positive	18	14	Personal need	13	15
Other	12	11	Impersonal	13	7
P	N.S.			N.S.	
Item 30			Item 43		
Long-range	12	18	Kibbutz – farming	8	2
Trivial	12	4	Studies	6	5
			Personality	15	13
P	< .03			N.S.	

Responses to the next two Guilt items present a fairly consistent picture in that the Kibbutz adolescents either deny or evade any admission of guilt.

To item 39 ("When I was younger I felt guilty in connection with . . .") a number of Kibbutz subjects simply state "I did not feel guilty" or give a non-specific (evasive) response, i.e., "something." Interpersonal and especially intrafamilial relations are reflected in the completions of the non-Kibbutz adolescents. When younger they felt guilty about attitudes to parents, "my brother," "my friend," etc. There were omissions on this item, but no outright denials or evasions. The trend is similar in the responses to item 52 ("The worst thing I did in my life . . ."). It is also interesting to note that 20 percent of the control group did not respond to this item at all. This latter fact, the outright denial of guilt and more reference to painful physical rather than moral situations on the part of the Kibbutz adolescents, all raise the question as to whether in fact Kibbutz youngsters really harbor less guilt than the controls.

The next two areas, Future and Goals, are quite similar in content for both deal with future perspective. One of the Future stems, item 30, ("One of these days, I . . .") highlights group differences quite clearly. The vast majority of the non-Kibbutz adolescents take this opportunity to state some fairly long-range goals ("build myself a farm," "shall be a member of a new colony," etc.). Fifty percent of the Kibbutz group respond in a similar manner, but the remainder mention rather trivial and relatively unimportant expectancies such as going on "an outing," "take a walk," etc. These results are quite similar to those obtained on the Goals item 29 ("My secret ambition in life . . ."). Aside from the desire of some Kibbutz subjects to leave the matter "secret" we note that most of them do not report any clear goals such as "to be a successful farmer" or "to be a literary man" which are reported by the majority of the non-Kibbutz group.

Some interesting differences are also reflected in the responses to two more items in the Goals area. Item 3 ("I always wanted to . . .") evokes rather different sets of responses; a large proportion of Kibbutz adolescents is interested in learning to "play the violin," "read good books," etc. Few control subjects express this desire; instead they emphasize again some vocational ambitions and long-range goals ("to be a pilot" or "study for a teacher," etc.). A variety of other wishes, some of them quite trivial, are expressed by both groups. On item 16 ("I would be definitely satisfied if . . .") group differences are also quite clear. Kibbutz adolescents show considerable interest in school (". . . if I am permitted to continue to study") and, again, ambition for some cultural accomplishments such as "playing the piano," "study art," and so on; this is much less true of the non-Kibbutz youngsters who refer to a miscellany of more practical needs ("our barn were better") and goals ("were able to be a pilot").

Sentences that deal with the Past produced relatively little meaningful material. Both groups responded in a similar fashion to "When I was a small child . . ." (item 8), describing early play activities and self-description. Item 21 ("Before the war I . . .") reveals some interesting differences insofar that a sizable number of Kibbutz adolescents convert it to a future reference. Thus, although the majority of both groups make some reference to past status ("I was a small child"), about a third of the Kibbutz group *expects* war and refer to plans prior to its possible outbreak (e.g., "I shall volunteer for the Army").

Greater nostalgia for the childhood period was noted in the Kibbutz group in response to item 34 ("If I were a small child again . . ."). Seven respondents thought it would be wonderful, e.g. "then I would return to the best period of my life," and three thought it "would not be good." The non-Kibbutz adolescents do not view the past either nostalgically or in negative terms; they would use hindsight ("then I would know what to do") to modify their behavior; most of them present noncommittal, neutral responses ("then I would be in kindergarten"). "My clearest childhood memory . . ." (item 47) shows some minor differences between the groups. Again, the Kibbutz respondents are more evasive; to a lesser extent their memories involve family and social experiences ("father goes to the Army"); and to a greater extent, personal events and experiences such as "a trip at night" or "my first philharmonic concert."

The last area to be included in the present section is that of

175

Abilities. As may be noted from the table, no statistically significant differences were obtained with any of the items in this area. Both groups respond in rather similar ways; this similarity, of course, is a function of the categorization of the responses, but the dissimilarities reported above are subject to the same restriction and criticism.

D. The area of sexuality

Two of the four items in this area differentiate between the groups with some degree of success. (*See* Table 7-7.) Responses to item 9 ("When I see a man and a woman together . . .") are of interest although the differences between the groups only approach statistical significance. Nearly half of the Kibbutz adolescents show some disturbance or involvement; "I laugh" or "There arise thoughts in me" are examples of this type of response. Most of the controls respond in a less involved fashion, in a matter-of-fact sort of manner ("I think it is a couple" or "I think they have something in common").

Table 7-7 Responses in the area of sex

	K	NK		K	NK
Item 9			Item 22		
Involvement	12	5	Happy	14	14
No involvement	13	16	Description	10	7
			Ambivalent	4	3
P		< .09			N.S.
Item 35			Item 48		
Discontinue-negative	14	5	Not yet	17	13
Positive-neutral	7	15	Some	4	5
P		< .02			N.S.

More marked and statistically significant are the differences in response to item 35 ("If I had sex relations . . ."). Here the attitude of the great majority of Kibbutz adolescents is quite clear; it is

176

negative. "I would discontinue," "not at my age," are examples of the type of response obtained. A clear-cut provisional rejection of heterosexual relations is obvious. Non-Kibbutz adolescents are less perturbed by such a possibility; "I would get married" or "I would be a father" were the types of response which characterized the majority of this group. Thus it would appear that sex taboos are much stronger for the Kibbutz group. This fact, in turn, may be responsible for greater suppression or repression of sexuality and, therefore, greater embarrassment and sensitivity to heterosexual social relations.

E. Summary

A number of interesting findings were gleaned from the responses to the 59 incomplete sentences. Statistically significant differences between the two groups of adolescents were obtained on 12 of these items (P equals .05 or less); results approaching statistical significance (P between the .05 and .10 levels) were achieved on seven more items. In addition, a number of items were not subjected to statistical tests of significance because of the small number in each category (cell); yet, mere inspection of the comparative figures contributes to our understanding of the trends in the data. We shall attempt to summarize the findings and present a composite picture of the major differences along the dimensions outlined.

As far as intrafamilial relationships are concerned, the two groups are similar in their reactions. Both groups tend to be more critical of the family, father and mother than are the ten year olds.

Some differences in *interpersonal relationships* were obtained and are of interest. Kibbutz adolescents "like best" people in their immediate environment who are closest to them; they do not tend to construct an abstract picture of the qualities of such people as do the controls. Friendship is dealt with more abstractly and is defined in terms of character and behavior rather than in terms of personal gain and assistance the presence of which, given their Kibbutz setting, they assume anyway. Similarly their dislikes are not directed against selfishness and snobbishness which are apparently rare in their egalitarian society. The work situation is a less personal one for the Kibbutz adolescent, whereas the opposite is true for the controls, who get along best with relatives and friends and depend upon their approval. This closer intrafamilial relationship in the workaday world probably makes the non-Kibbutz adolescent less respectful of leadership and causes him to place greater reliance upon himself and his immediate social milieu.

Kibbutz adolescents are particularly loath to admit the experience of fear. A miscellany of fears is mentioned by both groups, with Kibbutz adolescents less often mentioning death and darkness. Most interesting is the mode of handling fear which tends to be more active (problem solving and defensive) in the Kibbutz group and more passive (withdrawal and seeking help) in the non-Kibbutz group. With respect to guilt, it is hard to decide whether the Kibbutz adolescents actually do not experience it or are very defensive about it (deny, or evade). The former proposition is perhaps more defensible, for even when they do mention a desire to forget certain things, what they refer to is physical discomfort and objective anxiety.

With respect to time perspective and goals, it can be stated that Kibbutz adolescents tend to project a shorter time perspective, fewer long range goals and greater interest in pursuits that have a cultural and scholastic orientation rather than a vocational one.

Finally, sexuality is a rather touchy issue for Kibbutz adolescents. The hypothetical notion of heterosexual relations is rejected outright by the majority, at least for the "time being." This suppression (and/or repression), however, makes sexuality a sensitive area as indicated by our findings.

GENERAL SUMMARY

In summarizing the data presented in this chapter, we will deal with issues similar to those summarized at the end of the previous chapter. Since some of the techniques employed in the assessment of the adolescent groups are different from the ones used with the preadolescents the contents of this summary will differ, too. We shall not report on psychoanalytic variables for those were not studied specifically, but will include more information about fantasy content and its relevance to personality differences between the groups.

1. Intellectually, Kibbutz adolescents function at least as well and perhaps somewhat better than the controls. This trend is consistent with the findings obtained with the younger children, reported in Chapter 6.

2. With respect to overall "adjustment," no marked differences between the groups were noted; there were some maladjusted individuals in both groups. Some evidence of greater control and sublimation of primitive drives in the Kibbutz group was also elicited.

3. No differential findings with respect to anxiety were discerned. However, in handling of anxiety the trend is for the Kibbutz adolescents to either repress it or attack its source actively, whereas withdrawal and the seeking of help are more noticeable in the controls. There is also evidence to support the notion that Kibbutz adolescents are less conscious of, or ready to admit to, guilt feelings than are the controls.

4. Kibbutz adolescents are less intensely involved affectively with members of their family and evidence less conflict with them than do non-Kibbutz adolescents.

5. There is evidence of less strong personal ambition in terms of vocational or professional advancement in the Kibbutz group; yet, ambition in the direction of personal, cultural, and intellectual growth seems to be present to a higher extent than in the controls.

6. Non-Kibbutz adolescents tend to fantasy aggression more frequently; they identify with the aggressor. Kibbutz adolescents more often fantasy being the victims of aggression or they direct aggression against themselves (suicide).

7. In the area of sexuality there is evidence that the Kibbutz adolescent is more repressed and is consciously opposed to immature expressions in this area.

8.

Young Manhood:
The Army Samples

This chapter will deal with the fourth and final set of comparisons between Kibbutz and non-Kibbutz subjects. Fortunately, through the cooperation of Israel's army authorities, the author had access to the files of the Officers Selection Unit. These files contained a great deal of personal information and test data on all soldiers referred by their training units as potential officer material. The following sections will describe the random samples of Kibbutz and non-Kibbutz soldiers that were obtained, and the relevant measures on which they were compared. Subsequently, the results of the comparisons and their interpretation will be presented.

THE SAMPLES

The samples were drawn from among the soldiers who were referred to the Officers Selection Unit during the year 1954. In this unit the soldiers spent several days taking tests and participating in a variety of field problems and other situations similar to those employed by the OSS during World War II.

Our randomly selected samples consisted of 31 Kibbutz men and 31 men from non-Kibbutz rural settlements. The age range was from

18½ to 21 years. All but two of the Kibbutz sample completed 12 grades of schooling; the remaining two completed the 11th grade. The grade range for the non-Kibbutz group was wider—from grades 5 to 13. The median, however, was 11 grades.

Several questions in the general questionnaire, administered by the Officers Selection Unit, are of special interest. In the first place, all men were asked about their occupational aspirations. Table 8-1 summarizes the responses of those who answered this question—25

Table 8-1 Occupational area choices of the two groups

	Kibbutz	Non-Kibbutz
Military career	—	10
Agriculture-mechanics	10	8
Professional-artistic	2	7
"Kibbutz member"	13	—
Total	25	25

in each group. The remaining either did not respond or wrote "I don't know." It is interesting to note that, at least relatively early in their military service, none of the Kibbutz boys are interested in a military career. Forty percent of the non-Kibbutz respondents hope for a military career. Another aspect is the lack of concern of Kibbutz boys with professional careers. More than half of them stated simply that they were going to be "Kibbutz members," indicating no specific vocational or occupational plans. Underlying is the expectancy that they will do what is needed in the Kibbutz.

The final results of the selection process for these two parallel samples are also of interest. They lend statistical support to the impression of some of the officers I interviewed that the Kibbutz boys are good officer material. Perhaps the two facts are not altogether independent. At any rate, Table 8-2 summarizes the final disposition of the two groups by the selection committee which based its judgment on the pencil-and-paper tests, field tests and interviews.

Table 8-2 Results of the Officers Selection Unit

	Kibbutz	Non-Kibbutz	Chi^2	P
Accepted	13	9		
Rejected	10	20	8.07	< .02
"Not yet"	8	2		
Total	31	31		

We may note three categories in the table. Those "accepted" are considered officer material and are sent to officers training courses; the "rejected" are returned to their units to complete their 2½ year stint of compulsory military service; and, the third category consists of those who are not definitely rejected, but for reasons of immaturity and insufficient military experience are considered not yet ready. This last group will be again considered, at a later date, for the officers training course.

The distribution of the two samples in the three categories clearly points to the superiority of the Kibbutz group; more of them are definitely acceptable; fewer of them are clearly rejected; more of them still have a chance in future reconsideration.

Two additional sources of information, of a more formal nature, will serve as bases for comparison of the two groups: 1) Incomplete sentence test, and 2) The Thematic Apperception Test.

INCOMPLETE SENTENCES

Since the materials were not planned for or selected by the author, the incomplete sentences used for the soldiers are quite different from those of the younger groups. Moreover, it was necessary to select only relatively few incomplete sentences. The Officers Selection Unit had been experimenting with sveral forms of the sentence completion test; each form containing a different series of 60 incomplete sentences. But all forms had a common core of the following 12 stems:

1. I hope . . .
2. I am afraid . . .

3. The feeling of loneliness . . .
4. I don't feel well, when . . .

5. What bothers me most . . .   8. If only I could overcome . . .
6. I hate it when . . .   9. I can't function when . . .
7. When I am very annoyed   10. When I act on my own . . .
   (by others) . . .   11. In the group, generally . . .
    12. Pity . . .

Unlike the sentence completion material presented earlier, these stems do not readily fall into classifications. Most of them are stated in first person and deal with basic emotions, personality characteristics and interpersonal attitudes. The particular testing situation probably affected in no small measure the responses and hence, the results which were obtained.

We may now proceed to scrutinize the responses given by the two groups, sentence by sentence.

Item 1 ("I hope . . .") evoked many responses, in both groups, which reflect the situational effects. About one half of the total number of subjects is concerned with success on the tests and with admission to the officers training course (Table 8-3). However, a much smaller number of the Kibbutz group seem to be concerned with their military career—a finding consistent with the results obtained on the occupational questionnaire. Among the "miscellaneous" responses which are predominant in the Kibbutz group there are simpler, short-range concerns revealed. Five of the Kibbutz subjects hope for a visit home as compared with three of the non-Kibbutz group. The latter seem to be more involved in the testing situation as instrumental in their future military career. The differences between the groups approach statistical significance.

With respect to fear or anxiety (item 2), there seems to be no difference between the groups. About equal numbers in each group refer to internal stresses such as fear of failure to realize desired goals. A majority in both groups is concerned with environmental threats ("press") of a physical ("driving on a wet pavement") or social ("that the common project won't succeed") nature. There is also a fair number of trivial or evasive responses which are not infrequent to such a directly searching question.

183

Table 8-3 Comparison of sentence completions of Kibbutz (K) and Non-Kibbutz (NK) respondents

Sentence	Response classification	K	NK	Completion examples
1. I hope...	Pass test and be officer	10	18*	to be an officer
	Other	19	13	get home this week
2. I am afraid...	Personal failure or threat	11	12	that I won't succeed
	Environmental threat	18	17	of insults from others
3. The feeling of	Positive	4	1	gives satisfaction
loneliness...	Negative	18	19	depresses
	Denial (no bother)	5	5	does not bother me
4. I don't feel	Social discomfort	18	14	I am insulted
well when...	Physical discomfort	6	10	I am ill
5. What bothers	Internal factors	6	9	is nervousness
me most...	External factors	21	17	the noise and smoke
6. I hate it	Personal affront	19	10**	they yell at me
when...	Impersonal (injustice, impoliteness)	9	18	people neglect their duty
7. When I am very	Emotional reaction	22	14**	my blood boils
annoyed...	Avoidance	2	10	I laugh
	Mixed-ambivalent	5	5	I am angry and leave
8. If only I could	Personal weakness	14	7**	my shyness
overcome...	External handicap	6	12	the obstacles
9. I can't function	Social interference	19	15	people disturb me
when...	Personal reasons	7	6	I am very ill
	Circumstances	3	6	I have no means
10. When I act on	Successful; confident	20	15	I feel confidence
my own...	Doubt; failure	4	–	sometimes doubts are left
	Care and personal responsibility	3	9	it is my responsibility
11. In the group	Positive	23	19	I feel good
generally...	Ambivalent	5	10	there are different types
12. Pity...	Positive	8	14**	is a good trait
	Negative	15	6	is an ugly thing
	Ambivalent	6	9	is in itself no problem

*P < .07   **P = .05-.01

Perhaps somewhat related to anxiety is the sentence root "The feeling of loneliness . . ." (item 3). The vast majority of respondents in both groups consider it undesirable or depressing. A few in each group deny the negative aspects of loneliness; it does not bother *them*. Very few, however, attribute a downright positive value to loneliness indicating that they have a feeling of satisfaction in being alone; four Kibbutz subjects gave such a response, but only one of the non-Kibbutz group. It may be tempting to speculate that in the former case it reflects a reaction against the continuous group setting in which they have found themselves since infancy. The differences between the groups are, however, statistically not significant.

Again, no significant differences between the groups in response to item 4, "I don't feel well, when . . ." were obtained. The great majority of the Kibbutz sample mentioned a variety of social pressures and unpleasantness ("the group doesn't want me," "I am laughed at," etc.). A slimmer majority of the parallel group mentioned similar situations, while a larger number of the same group, compared with the Kibbutz, mentioned physical discomfort and indisposition (i.e., "I have a temperature"). The only two responses which refer to the discomfort of a friend as a cause of their own not feeling well were given by Kibbutz subjects.

Item 5 ("What bothers me most . . ."), which is somewhat related to item 4, also does not elicit any significant differences. Majorities of both groups are disturbed by external factors and circumstances, physical and social. A closer analysis of the "external" factors reveals that some differences exist within this classification. Whereas eight Kibbutz subjects mention bad social attitudes (i.e., "suspicion and lack of trust"), only four of the non-Kibbutz subjects show a similar concern. More of the latter emphasize physical factors and other "conditions."

More clear-cut differences between the groups appear on item 6 ("I hate it when . . ."). Personal affront is most mentioned by the Kibbutz subjects, whereas the non-Kibbutz individuals consider more often rather impersonal situations, often involving injustices visited upon others (i.e., "hitting the weak"). In this context it would appear that the Kibbutz group is more egocentric. The differ-

185

ences between the groups are statistically significant at a respectable level of confidence.

Significant differences are also elicited by item 7 ("When I am very annoyed . . ."). The Kibbutz subjects readily admit their emotional reaction in the situation; they "get angry," "get heated" and are "capable of anything." A sizeable number of the non-Kibbutz group claims to utilize a frequently employed defense—"I laugh." This is more than avoidance; it is a sort of reaction formation of certain cultural origins. Interestingly enough, one of the non-Kibbutz subjects remarked: "I learned this from the British." The directness of emotional reaction and relative lack of diplomacy of the Kibbutz subjects tends to be consistent with the egocentric trend mentioned for item 6.

Item 8 ("If I could only overcome . . .") elicits some information which is relevant to some of the characteristics of the Kibbutz subjects alluded to in the previous section. Omitting a miscellany of trivial responses, we are left with a dichotomy of the need for change in the self vs. the overcoming of external conditions or handicaps. The majority of the dichotomized responses of the Kibbutz group fall in the "self-control" category. The difference in the incidence of these two categories of response between the two groups is statistically significant. Attempting to integrate this finding with the trends toward direct emotional reaction, we may state that the Kibbutz subjects recognize their affect, find it disturbing and are concerned more with its control or "elimination."

Despite the wish to "overcome" certain personal weaknesses, there is no indication that these are the most important causes in malfunctioning, dealt with in item 9 ("I can't function when . . ."). Here the vast majority of responses do not refer to personal shortcomings, but to social interference and a variety of other unfavorable conditions. There are no marked differences between the two groups on this item. In attempting to integrate the results on item 9 with those of item 8, we may consider two possibilities: 1) that the personal shortcomings which the Kibbutz subjects wish to overcome are not perceived as interfering in their functioning adequately; and that, 2) perhaps, there is a projection onto the group of the failure to function adequately and lack of admission of personal short-comings; however, this possibility could be considered with both groups and not with the Kibbutz group exclusively.

For a variety of reasons, the issue of "independent functioning" in our comparisons is of considerable interest. How do Kibbutz-reared young men, i.e., persons reared from infancy as group members, feel about acting as independent individuals? In response to item 10 which taps this issue ("When I act on my own . . ."), we note a larger proportion of Kibbutz respondents reporting positive feelings and feelings of success and confidence. However, several Kibbutz subjects also report doubt and fear of failure in this context ("I have some doubts left at times")—a type of response entirely absent in the non-Kibbutz group. Subjects in the latter group emphasize more caution and the feeling of personal responsibility as well as the dislike for interference by others. It is also of interest that two Kibbutz respondents referred to their independent actions as a source of annoyance or even harm to their friends or the group. There seems to be a greater trend of ambivalence about independent functioning in this group.

A feeling of comfort and ease in the group situation is reflected in the responses of a larger proportion of the Kibbutz group—item 11 ("In the group, generally . . ."). A greater proportion of soldiers in the non-Kibbutz group respond with ambivalence or see downright negative features in the group situation (e.g., "the weak suffer and the strong become conspicuous").

Finally, somewhat puzzling results were obtained with item 12 ("Pity . . ."). Table 8-3 shows quite clearly the difference in the incidence of responses between the groups (which is statistically significant). The Kibbutz majority considers "pity" an undesirable emotion whereas almost the opposite is true of the non-Kibbutz group. One of the latter group writes of pity as "the mother of generosity and of positive activity!" Few of the Kibbutz group are as unreservedly positive about it. For them, pity is an insult to the dignity of the individual.

In an attempt to explain this dominant attitude toward pity in the Kibbutz group, two main possibilities may be considered: 1)

187

The unequivocal rejection of pity as an undesirable emotion may be understood by way of some of the ambivalent responses, such as "it is a good feeling in many cases, but also disturbing." In other words, this "disturbing" aspect of pity is being rejected and/or defended against; 2) In Kibbutz ideology which glorifies the group and emphasizes the equality among individuals, pity is conceived of as a threat to that equality; it involves a separation of the weak from the strong.

Summary

In pulling together the bits of data and response trends we have to cope with the heterogeneity of the material. Nevertheless, a composite picture of the differences between the Kibbutz and non-Kibbutz groups will be attempted.

There is some clustering of items which focus on several general personality attributes; five categories evolve: 1) feelings of anxiety, 2) emotional reactivity, 3) self-control and defensive measures, 4) the group and social interaction, and 5) goals and aspirations.

The area of anxiety, as reflected in the sentence completion technique employed, is not one in which sharp differences between the two groups are noted. Quantitatively and qualitatively the differences do not appear to be of great significance. Items 2, 3, 4, 5 and 9 serve as a basis for this judgment. The only trends that may qualify the statement are the indications that a few more Kibbutz subjects see positive value in being alone, i.e., a smaller proportion of them are uncomfortable with the "feeling of loneliness." And, for the Kibbutz group, the sources of discomfort (anxiety?) are more often of social origin, i.e., disapproval and rejection by other individuals or by the group. This notion is reinforced by the trend revealed in item 9, which deals with interference with functioning.

As far as emotional reactivity is concerned, items 6 and 7 are primarily involved. We have already mentioned the directness with which the Kibbutz group admits its reaction to frustration. There is relatively little defensiveness about it. They freely admit emotional reactions when being "annoyed" or when subjected to a personal

188

affront or attack. The non-Kibbutz group, in a way, appears to be more "sophisticated" in this respect. They tend to sublimate in response to item 6 by displacing their hatred to more impersonal behavior and, in response to item 7, they tend to use more frequently reaction formation ("laughing") in coping with annoyance.

In considering item 8, which deals directly with self-control, we note again the relative directness and, perhaps, lack of defensiveness of the Kibbutz group. Members of this group tend to admit quite readily that they wish to "overcome" personal weakness. The implication here is a wish for conscious control or suppression. At the same time, the admission of the personal shortcomings implies relatively conscious anxiety about them and also, probably, the relative lack of success in attempts to alter the condition. It may be supposed that a greater degree of introspection, self-reflection and self-criticism is involved. In dealing with "pity" (item 12), additional information concerning the defensive patterns of the groups may be inferred. If, as Fenichel (1945) states, "the suspicion is confirmed often (that) . . . sadism actually is found behind the facade of pity" (p. 476), then the non-Kibbutz group which accepts pity as a positive reaction more frequently exhibits greater tendencies toward reaction formation against the sadistic impulses. The Kibbutz group, on the other hand, to a large extent rejects pity as an undesirable mode of behavior. By implication, it has less need for defense against hostility and sadism; unless we consider this trend as a "defense against a defense" for which we do not have any evidence at hand.

Of particular interest are the relationships of members of our two samples to the group. As might be expected, the proportion of Kibbutz subjects who feel comfortable in the group setting is greater than among the controls (item 11). On the other hand, responses on item 10 indicate greater numbers of the Kibbutz group feel confident when functioning independently "on my own." This apparent inconsistency with item 11 is resolved when we discuss the differences in the wording between them. The Kibbutz subjects feel comfortable when they *are* in the group (item 11), but some of them are beset by doubt and fear of failure when acting on their own (item

189

10). This would indicate an excessive degree of dependency on the part of those subjects. Such a trend, however, is absent in the non-Kibbutz subjects.

We may again point out that the hopes and aspirations of the Kibbutz group seem to be less situational—less in the direction of a military career for which they were being tested. Most of them conceive of their future along the lines of the perpetuation of the Kibbutz. Whether the prolonged separation from the "home base" and years of army experience may modify this attitude is a question which cannot be answered at this point.

THE TAT DATA

Unfortunately TAT material was not available for all of the subjects in the Army samples. Not all the officer candidates wrote stories, nor did the ones who wrote stories deal with the same pictures. We were able to rescue some data from the files, however. The stories pulled were to cards, 4, 6B and 17BM. Results reported below are based on 16 to 21 Kibbutz stories but only on 7 to 8 non-Kibbutz stories. Admittedly this is rather meager material but the trends obtained make it worthwhile to include them in our report.

Let us consider the heroes and the themes in Card 4. With the exception of the reversal of trend in the identification of the heroes, when compared with the result reported on the adolescents, there is nothing special about these data.

A larger proportion of the Kibbutz young men identify the couple in the picture as "husband and wife"; the reverse was true about the stories of the adolescents. It is in the themes that we note the reversal of trend even more markedly. In Table 8-4 the reported proportions indicate that the Kibbutz young men produced relatively few stories in which the major theme was that of aggression (intended or actual), with the woman attempting to prevent it. More than half of the non-Kibbutz stories project this theme. On the other hand, infidelity and promiscuity feature prominently in a sizable percentage of Kibbutz stories and are represented to a negligible extent in the productions of the small sample of non-Kibbutz young men. Again, this is a perfect reversal of the trend obtained with the two groups of adolescents. It may be speculated that, perhaps, after the Kibbutz youngsters left the confines and supervision of the Kibbutz community their fantasy with respect to heterosexual relationships ranges quite far afield. The change in trend of the non-Kibbutz group is not so readily explained, and of course, the size of this sample is so small that any trend becomes highly tentative.

Table 8-4 Characteristics of the TAT stories of the two groups (percentages of incidence)

Heroes	K	NK	Themes	K	NK	Outcome	K	NK
Card 4								
Husband and wife	38	29	Aggression	12	57			
Lovers	25	29	Infidelity — promiscuity	57	14			
Other & unspecified	37	42	Love — reunion	19	28	—		
			Other	12	—			
Card 6 BM								
Woman & son	82	63	Separation	38	—			
			Death (child — father)	38	50	—		
Other	18	37	Other	24	50			
Card 17 BM								
Prisoner — criminal	43	—	Escape from prison	26	—	Favorable	37	28
Acrobat	14	43	Performance	26	57	Unfavorable	42	28
Soldier	14	—	Emergency	21	14	Uncertain	21	43
Other	29	57	Other	26	29			

Card 6BM stimulated some stories which manifest some interesting group contrasts. Since this card was not employed with the adolescents, its description and the latent stimulus demand as presented by Henry (1956) are in order.

Card 6BM. "A short elderly woman stands with her back turned to a tall young man. The latter is looking downward with a perplexed expression." Henry suggests that "This card deals most generally

191

with the attitudes of the subject toward maternal figures . . . the breaking of the relationship reflects ability to activate new ideas and projects . . . a good portrayal of the subjects' degree of independence is given."

The vast majority of Kibbutz subjects identified the pair in the picture as mother and son; the remainder as mother and the son's friend or comrade in arms. Fewer non-Kibbutz subjects made a similar identification. Some of them saw a woman and a doctor reporting about the illness of a member of the family. In the latter case it would seem that an attempt was made to avoid dealing with the mother-son relationship.

Separation is a major theme in the Kibbutz stories. The young man departs from his mother; in some stories with her approval, and in some without it. This theme is entirely absent in the non-Kibbutz stories. Kibbutz young men apparently project less dependence upon maternal authority and a greater degree of autonomy than do their peers reared in the nuclear family setting. In the remaining stories the death of a member of the family and its announcement by a son are quite common in both groups. There are some differences of significance in the last category ("other") which contains some stories of conflict between mother and son. Even in these stories, the resolution of the conflict in the direction of the son's independence is more prominent in the Kibbutz stories.

The third, and last, of the TAT cards of these samples is 17BM. Nearly half of the Kibbutz young men tell stories involving activist conditions—escape to liberty or committing criminal and emergency acts, such as spying, sabotage etc. Not so the controls. Some of their stories are aimless, without any specific direction or purpose, ("just climbing a rope"); other stories involve acrobats— exhibition and performance. For the Kibbutz young men the performance theme is not so important. Theirs is a more militant type of attitude to the external environment.

Drive control

An analysis of the "drive control" similar to the one reported for the stories of the adolescents (Chapter 7) was made on the basis of stories to two cards written by these groups. Results of this analysis are presented in Table 8-5.

Table 8-5 Comparison of "drive control" on two TAT cards (number of stories)

Dominant level	Card 4		Card 6 BM	
	K	NK	K	NK
Level I (direct-unsocialized)	7	2	4	1
Level II (direct-socialized)	7	5	17	7
Level III (indirect-disguised)				
Differences not significant				

Though the proportion of stories written by Kibbutz young men (in response to card 4) that show a predominance of "direct-unsocialized" drive is greater than that found on the non-Kibbutz group, the differences are not significant. Neither are there any notable group differences in the stories to card 6BM. This is in marked contrast to the results obtained with the adolescents, where, on both cards, the Kibbutz subjects consistently exhibited greater drive control than the non-Kibbutz group. It is difficult to account for the differences between the Kibbutz adolescents and young men. Instead of a "maturing" trend they show a reverse trend. Perhaps Kibbutz adolescence is less stormy, less conflict- and drive-ridden. Then, "a delayed reaction" may take place when the young man is catapulted into the wider "outside" world, represented by the Army.

TAT SUMMARY

Whereas repression (or suppression) of sexuality was evident in the findings with Kibbutz adolescents, the Kibbutz young men tend to project preoccupation with this issue. The fact that the fantasy productions emphasize infidelity and promiscuity may be an

193

indication of the continued mistrust with which heterosexual relationship is regarded.

Greater freedom from maternal authority seems to characterize the stories of the Kibbutz sample; whenever there is conflict between mother and son its resolution is accomplished by the son. Quite frequently, however, his autonomy is obtained without difficulty and conflict and with the blessings of the mother. In other words, mothers are often seen as not insisting on the perpetuation of the mother-son dependency; the trend seems to be in the opposite direction in the material obtained from the non-Kibbutz subjects.

Whereas the environment is viewed by the controls as relatively benign and appreciative of individual performance and achievement, it is viewed by the Kibbutz group as cramping, unjust and calling for rebellion and activism in the interest of a personal or social cause.

The comparative advantage of the Kibbutz group (over the non-Kibbutz group during adolescence) in the ability to channelize drive more adequately does not appear to be maintained.

General Summary

If selection for officers training courses is to be considered as an index of ego strength and overall adjustment and adaptability, then it can be said that the Kibbutz young men do quite well when compared with the controls. This external criterion supports the trend stated previously for Kibbutz children and adolescents that subsequent to the period of infancy the Kibbutz subjects make an adequate adjustment.

Some further conclusions, stemming from comparisons between the groups, and from consistencies and inconsistencies with earlier trends, may be warranted.

1. Less aggression and hostility is generally projected in the materials obtained from Kibbutz subjects. The more militant vigilant attitude to the environment is maintained. Personal autonomy and early withdrawal from parental control are also noted.

2. Findings, which are somewhat inconsistent with those ob-

tained with the younger groups, point to relatively reduced impulse control and increased concern with heterosexuality and promiscuity in the Kibbutz young men.

3. Additional trends for the Kibbutz man are his greater comfort in, and dependency upon, the group and his more frequent ambivalence about independent functioning. More complex defense mechanisms, such as reaction formation, are less readily available to Kibbutz subjects in anxiety-provoking situations.

4. The Kibbutz young men do not rebel against their society; on the contrary, they feel rooted in it, expect to return to it following military service, and perpetuate its collective values in preference to individual plans and ambitions.

9.

Summing Up

In the preceding chapters we have presented the results which highlighted the differences between Kibbutz and non-Kibbutz subjects at several age levels. These differences are along a number of different dimensions of personality development and adjustment. It would be well, in concluding this presentation, to summarize briefly and attempt to integrate the mass of findings and the piecemeal conclusions which have been drawn from them. Before doing this, we shall restate some of the questions we have raised originally and for which answers have been sought in the data and findings obtained.

Effects of "Partial Deprivation"

In chapter 3 we have compared the conditions of child rearing in the Kibbutz with those found in institutions and in the typical nuclear family setting. It was noted that Kibbutz child rearing, especially in the earlier years, may be placed in a position midway between the extremes of the family and the traditional institution. On the one hand the Kibbutz has some of the institutional *shortcomings;* on the other hand it may be characterized by some of the advantages offered by the typical family.

Using Goldfarb's (1955) schema, we have pointed out that with respect to the "warmth and intensity of adult emotional response" and "adult approval and reward" and with respect to the "richness of environmental stimulation" the Kibbutz child's environment is comparable with that of the family child.

However, the continuity and specificity of adult-child relationships, the immediacy in the gratification of tensions in infancy, the "number of children per adult," and the stereotypy of the environment are areas in which a degree of similarity to conditions existing in institutions may be noted. These aspects prompted us to term the situation of the Kibbutz child as one of *partial maternal* and/or psychologic deprivation.

We shall now address ourselves to those issues which have been highlighted in studies of the consequences of maternal deprivation as it occurs mainly under conditions of continuous institutionalization (Bowlby, 1951).

First, let us deal with the issue of intellectual retardation. Apparently the first year of life is about the most difficult one for the child in the Kibbutz setting. Our findings for the Kibbutz child indicate that some retardation in locomotor, speech and hearing (social response), and hand-eye coordination areas is present, but most important is his deficiency in the area of responses to other humans in the environment. There seems to be a lag, particularly in the development of basic trust in other human beings, perhaps primarily due to the lack of continuity in object relationships.

There is probably a concomitant lag in the clear conceptualization of significant figures in the environment. The change in the metapelet that takes place at the end of the first year is an additional instance of discontinuity, that may even be traumatic in some instances.

This is as far as we can go with the deprivation hypothesis. The next issue is that of the long-range effects of this experience. Here we take a long step along the temporal dimension—from the first year to the ten year olds.

The relative developmental retardation noted in the Kibbutz infants is not maintained in later years. The ten year olds, the adolescents and the young men of the Army, all give evidence that they are not retarded as compared with the control groups. On the contrary, some of the evidence, especially on the ten year olds and the adolescents, indicates greater developmental advances of the Kibbutz groups as compared with the non-Kibbutz peers. (To be sure, our data are cross-sectional, they are not longitudinal; we are not dealing with the *same* children who were examined as infants.) Because of our jump from one to ten years, we do not know at what point the rise in the Kibbutz child's developmental curve reaches or intersects the non-Kibbutz child's curve and becomes closely parallel to it. Further investigation of children between these ages might pinpoint the period of recovery.

A second issue relating to the consequences of deprivation is the "capacity for inhibition" or self-control. This is an ego function that is very essential in the process of adjustment and adaptation to reality. No methods specifically concerned with this characteristic were included in our research design. However, the methods we employed give us information that is relevant to this issue.

Most of the information concerning the capacity for inhibition in the ten year olds is derived from the Rorschach. In addition to the indirect evidence stemming from ratings of adequate ego strength, level of personality maturity and indices of overall adjustment, some more direct data were also obtained. We found that the control of form (F) over affectivity (C) is considerably better for the Kibbutz ten year olds than for the non-Kibbutz children.

Similar, although less marked, differences on the Rorschach, were obtained when the two groups of adolescents were compared. Moreover, a specific index of "drive control" derived from the TAT quite significantly points to the superiority of the Kibbutz group in this respect.

Although the index of drive control does not hold up with the group of young men (Army sample), the differences do not indicate any inferiority of the Kibbutz subjects. Moreover, using an indirect index, i.e., selection for officers training courses on the basis of psychological and situational (field problems) tests, the Kibbutz young men show up better, by far, than the members of the non-Kibbutz group. Certainly, drive control is a significant ingredient in the ability to pass and perform according to the grueling demands of the testing situation described.

Thus, our conservative conclusion should be that Kibbutz-reared children, adolescents, and young men demonstrate at least as much capacity for drive control as do the parallel non-Kibbutz groups.

Among the other consequences of early deprivation we find a variety of behavioral and personality characteristics, listed by Bowl-by (1951) and later summarized by Goldfarb (1955). We shall not concern ourselves with the more strictly behavioral aspects (e.g., hyperactivity, restlessness, etc.) which depend entirely upon direct impressions and observations of overt activity. Such material is extremely difficult to rate and quantify. We may obtain, however, inferences from our data with respect to such more covert personality characteristics as "superficial affectivity," "absence of guilt feelings" and "defect in social maturity."

There are some lines of evidence that relate to intensity and depth of affectional relationships and attachments. On the one hand, the Kibbutz youngsters demonstrate lower Oedipal intensity than their non-Kibbutz counterparts. From this we may infer weaker emotional relationships and attachments within the biological family circle. However, whether this is an indication of an incapacity for "genuine emotional attachments" is, to a degree, a matter of semantics. We do have evidence of positive attitudes to parents and to the family, although we do not have any evidence concerning the intensity of these attitudes. We may obtain some further relevant evidence from the contents of the TAT material. The sample responses to cards 3 BM and 10 are indicative of depth in emotional attachment and intensity of interpersonal relationship (*see* Chapter 7). There are many other instances that could not be quantified but point in the same direction. Thus, the information remains tentative and inconclusive.

As to guilt feelings, our data (on the sentence completion and TAT) do not reveal any important differences between the Kibbutz and non-Kibbutz groups. Subjects of both groups admit to the experience of guilt—the ten year olds as well as the adolescents. On the sentence completion, the Kibbutz adolescents tend to deny (or evade?) more often the experience of guilt.

There is also some evidence that the contents of the guilt feelings in the two groups may differ. Whereas, at least on the TAT, Kibbutz guilt more often involves sexuality, non-Kibbutz guilt is concerned with hostility and aggression. Although no precise measurements of intensity are available, perusal of the data would support the notion that guilt is present in both groups, but that the intensity is higher in the non-Kibbutz group.

Our findings would certainly not support the notion of social immaturity which is alleged to be a consequence of maternal deprivation. Ratings of overall maturity based on the Rorschach point to a higher level obtained by the Kibbutz subjects. Moreover, a comparison of socialized versus unsocialized drive control, based on the data obtained with the Kibbutz and non-Kibbutz adolescents and Army samples (with the TAT), lends no support to social maturity being less among Kibbutz children. With the adolescents, a larger incidence of socialized drive control is found in the Kibbutz group; the Army samples show no significant differences. It would be fair to conclude that our Kibbutz subjects are at least as well off with respect to social maturity as their age peers in the ordinary community setting. This is not surprising, for the Kibbutz children are raised in groups, and taught group living and cooperation, from a rather tender age.

Thus, it may be stated that the predictions based on the maternal deprivation hypothesis with respect to personality characteristics do not hold for the children who grow up under the Kibbutz conditions of collective education. The only possible exception to this is that the intensity of guilt tends to be lower in the Kibbutz samples—a trend consonant with the conclusions based on Spiro's (1958) observations.

ADJUSTMENT, PERSONALITY STRUCTURE AND PSYCHODYNAMICS

The issues to be considered here overlap to a considerable degree the ones just discussed—the predictions made with respect to consequences of deprivation are to a large extent related to adjustment and personality structure. In the present context we shall deal with an array of variables and comparisons that go beyond the predicted consequences of the nonconventional mother-child relationship.

Clinically, adjustment is often considered to be the absence of signs of maladjustment. The judgment of signs of maladjustment

200

or symptoms of emotional disturbance is often highly qualitative and nonobjective and, to some degree, dependent upon cultural norms and standards. This we have discussed in Chapter 3. Our present assessment of adjustment is based on inferences made from more or less objective measures of personality and personality structure on which Kibbutz and non-Kibbutz subjects were compared.

Some emotional maladjustment in the Kibbutz infants and toddlers was reported in Chapter 5 which dealt with "early development." This conclusion stems from two sources: 1) the discrepancy between the low achievement in the personal-social area as compared with the other areas of the developmental scale, and 2) the evidence of withdrawal and other signs of emotional maladjustment obtained from the history material on these infants.

Here again, the picture changes completely when we focus on the ten year olds. The indices of general adjustment based on the Rorschach, independent ratings of "levels of personality maturity" (based on Rorschach summaries) and variables of ego development, all point up a sharp reversal of the trend noted with the infants. The Kibbutz ten year olds are judged to be at least as mature, as well developed intellectually and emotionally and, generally, as well adjusted as their peers in the ordinary family setting. In most instances, the indices we have employed even point to the superiority of the Kibbutz children in these areas.

The trend is maintained for the adolescents. Adjustment indices, based on the Rorschach, and drive control indices (socialized vs. unsocialized drives) based on the TAT, again point up the relative adequacy of our Kibbutz sample.

There is also some further "indirect" evidence that the level of adequate adjustment is maintained beyond the period of adolescence. The main indirect source is the relative success of a randomly selected sample of Kibbutz soldiers in making the grade by being chosen for the Officers training courses. Certainly emotional stability and adjustment is, by implication, one of the important selective criteria for leadership positions in any army.

We note, again, that despite his problematic start the Kibbutz child from age ten onward, progresses quite adequately, as far as his overall emotional adjustment is concerned. And again, we do not yet know at what point between the ages of one and ten years the direction has been reversed. Most likely it is not a "point" but a "phase" of corrective experience and development.

Any discussion of personality structure is of necessity related to predictions made, and tested, on the basis of psychodynamic theory and the concept of ego which is rather central in this theory. Assessment of ego adequacy at different age levels has been very much the focus of our investigation. It was noted earlier that something was amiss with the coping mechanisms and early ego development of the Kibbutz infant. A number of circumstances in the child rearing situation may be responsible for this, primarily, it would seem, the excessive amount of frustration to which the infant is exposed in the Kibbutz nursery. His wants are not immediately and "magically" gratified by environmental agents. This is so especially at night when adults are scarce and cannot respond as swiftly to the infant's demands as a parent in the ordinary family setting. Even during the day, when the biological mother is not around, the response of the metapelet who has several other children under her care is not always "immediate." Hence, the amount of frustration experienced by the infant may exceed his as yet undeveloped capacity to tolerate frustration, to bind anxiety.

Still another issue may be crucial—the discontinuity in adult-child interaction. We do not have "separation" in the sense discussed in the maternal deprivation literature. From the very beginning, the Kibbutz child has two maternal figures—the biological mother and the metapelet. The alternation of the two in the care of the infant, prior to the age of six months or so, is perhaps of little consequence. Subsequent to that age, however, when recognition usually takes place and the anticipation of a specific figure develops, the Kibbutz infant has a more difficult task than the child in the ordinary family. The latter discriminates between mother and non-mother. The Kibbutz child, because the source of his gratification is lodged in two maternal figures, has to make more complex discriminations, i.e., between mother A, mother B and non-mother. Moreover, the anticipatory behavior and reaction pattern of the child may often be confused and mistaken for it is not always clear which mother will appear to ease the tensions. As a result, we find a temporary withdrawal of ego and a retardation in ego development; the child's perceptual, executive, and integrative mechanisms are too immature and insufficiently developed to cope with the frustrations.

The generally positive, accepting and rewarding adult environment soon aids the Kibbutz toddler in sorting out his perceptions and in organizing his specific reaction patterns. Frustration is no longer excessive; gratification from a widening array of sources returns to the infant the basic trust in the environment. The stage is then set for maturation of the conflict-free ego (Hartmann, 1958).

The process of socialization during the toddler period still remains more demanding for the Kibbutz child than for his non-Kibbutz peer. In spite of a progressive and permissive attitude on the part of the metapelet and in spite of the daily visits to his biological family, the socialization demands on the Kibbutz child are extensive in view of the nearly constant presence of several age peers in the immediate environment. Curbing aggression, learning to cooperate, share and participate with the group, represent an additional burden upon the fragile ego. Thus, it may be hypothesized that not only the first year but the first three or four years are extremely difficult for the Kibbutz child. He has to develop skills and controls, especially in the interpersonal area, that are required at a considerably later age of the child who grows up in the ordinary family setting. By the time the Kibbutz child has reached Kindergarten or school age he has been through many of the battles which the non-Kibbutz child has yet to face. He is freer to meet the demands of the educational program. It is, probably, then that the spurt in development of the Kibbutz child begins.

Before we proceed with the discussion of personality structure, it is necessary to deal with some of the predictions and findings based on psychodynamic theory. Essentially we have found that the children of the Kibbutz show lower Oedipal intensity than the controls. The less intense attachment to the parent of the opposite sex and the less ambivalent relationship and attitude to the parent of the same sex are conducive to normal, non-neurotic personality development.

Bettelheim's (1962) speculations on this issue are quite consonant with our findings. It is interesting to note that a lesser Oedipal intensity does not detract from the positive attitudes revealed by the Kibbutz children to both parents. A further consequence of this Oedipal situation, however, is the less clear-cut identification of the Kibbutz child with the same-sex parent. Identification is more diffuse than in the control group; the parent of the same sex is not necessarily the chosen model for introjection; the identification is less decisive, for the anxiety underlying it is either absent or less severe and less threatening in the case of the Kibbutz child. It is for this reason that the superego is less severe and less punitive. This finding is to some degree supported by our data and also by Spiro's (1958) observations.

Aside from the lesser intensity of guilt, which we have mentioned in connection with the discussion of partial deprivation, some additional concepts related to what might be termed "ego ideal" should be considered: the concepts of time perspective and time orientation (Wallace and Rabin, 1960). In a number of instances, in the previous chapters, when responses to Future and Goals items on the sentence completion test were considered we noted distinct differences between the Kibbutz and non-Kibbutz children. The former were either primarily present-oriented or demonstrated brief future time perspective and interest in more immediate goals; the latter, the controls, were more future-oriented, indicated longer future time perspectives and extended, long-range goals. It is difficult to say, however, whether this is an instance of a basic personality characteristic, i.e., a preference for more immediate gratification; or, whether it is an extra-personality factor (of a more superficial nature) due to the social structure of the Kibbutz where long-range personal aspirations for the future are unrealistic in view of the individual's dependence upon group or corporate decisions.

That the relative lack of concern with distant personal goals and ambitions is not a fundamental character defect, which might be due to an inability to postpone gratification, is supported by two sources of evidence. First, we have noted that the Kibbutz children and adolescents tend to be concerned with the development of their personality attributes and educational attainments outside any formal mold, since this is not provided by their society. Secondly, they are concerned with the more distant future and distant goals in the framework of the collectivity; hopes and aspirations for Kibbutz, country and world are more often expressed by Kibbutz youngsters. Thus, much of what might seem impulsive in character (immediate vs. delayed gratification) is actually a characteristic primarily dependent upon the culture's supply of molds in which personal expectancies, aspirations and anticipations may be formed.

There is still another consideration. Scattered throughout the previous chapters are occasional comments about the greater pessimism that tends to be projected in the material obtained from Kibbutz-reared subjects. It may well be that a general pessimistic attitude plays a significant role in foreshortening the future time perspective. There is a concomitance here, that is, a correlation or congruence between phenomena rather than a cause and effect relationship. Perhaps some of the antecedent circumstances and child-rearing experiences are at the root of both of these aspects—pessimism and limited future time perspective. Although the early infancy which is fraught with frustration, does not leave any important mark upon ego development and general emotional stability, it may well be that this period is important in delineating a general attitude—pessimism—which may be an integral aspect of character structure and personality development. Our inclination, in viewing these trends, is to point to 1) the relatively greater cultural influence in the limited future time perspective and 2) the more personal, psychological and experiential-developmental origins in the pessimism.

With respect to the more specific and related issue of goals and personal ambition a few more words are in order. Kibbutz children are not devoid of ambition or lacking in goals involving self-development and self-realization. They lack, however, the knowledge of appropriate social and cultural forms for the channeling of these ambitions, forms that Kibbutz society has not yet adequately provided, but which are readily available to the child in the larger, open society.

THE DRIVES

Some observers of the Kibbutz scene have emphasized the alleged high degree of hostility in Kibbutz children (e.g., Spiro, 1958). In view of the fact that we compared Kibbutz children with other Israeli children we cannot subscribe to such an absolute judgment. The evidence is not entirely unequivocal on this point. The ten year olds among the Kibbutz children studied indicate high incidence of "anal sadism" directed against parental figures, as compared with the non-Kibbutz controls. This is the only instance in which the Kibbutz children's hostility is higher. In all other instances the fantasies projected point to comparatively less hostility in Kibbutz children. Sibling rivalry is markedly lower. The fantasy of the Kibbutz child, when it does project aggression, tends to exclude the personal motive and to direct aggression into group effort and struggle, such as war and revolution. Also, aggression directed against the self, in the form of suicide, is more common in Kibbutz fantasy productions. Thus, hostility is either socially sanctioned and channeled or it is directed inward, trends that would make the personal expression of hostility and aggression toward other individuals less likely.

In the fantasy material of non-Kibbutz adolescents, hostility and aggression are often interwoven with heterosexuality. Sexuality *per se* is less repressed in this group than in the Kibbutz subjects. The Kibbutz adolescents seem to be highly tempted by and concerned with sex, but they suppress it, mainly for ideological reasons and because of the external social pressure in the Kibbutz setting. However, it appears that the controls of heterosexuality become more relaxed when the Kibbutz youngster enters the Army where his ideology is not so salient and where the external social controls of the Kibbutz recede.

THE ISSUE OF CONFORMITY

Some of the participants in the symposium at which Caplan (1954) originally described Kibbutz child rearing raised the issues of uniformity and conformity with regard to the products of collective education. They asked essentially: "Does not Kibbutz education

206

produce a sort of homogenized personality? Are not all the children alike in character and personality structure because of the similarity in their infantile experiences?"

In response to these questions it must be stated that they imply a wrong premise, and that the final answer to them is an emphatic "no." The incorrect assumption is that the early (and later) environment of the Kibbutz child is so uniform and stereotyped that the product does not vary greatly. In reality, the early interaction of the infant with his peers in the nursery and toddlers house, with his parents and metapelet and, subsequently, with biological siblings, during the daily visits to the parental quarters, provide a great degree of variability in the interpersonal and physical environment. Later, the child is open to a broader range of influences extending to the friendly, and frequently doting, Kibbutz membership. The obvious fact that the children are different genetically, with different *Anlagen* and reactivities to environmental stimuli, is a further argument against the assumption of the uniformity hypothesis.

In addition to rejecting the premise, one should look at the data obtained, the distribution of the psychometric responses and the fantasy productions. To be sure, we do not possess a quantitative index of originality and variability, but mere inspection of the range and distribution of the responses and of the various indices based upon them points to tremendous variability in content as well as in personality structure of the Kibbutz youngsters. This observation does not in any way invalidate our conclusions about some congruity in character and its structure. We are talking about group trends and central tendencies that have high probabilities of occurrence in the Kibbutz, as we would study national character or modal personalities. The inference from similarities between members of a group, along a limited number of dimensions, is not equivalent to saying that the individuals are devoid of uniqueness. The nomothetic approach does not imply a denial of the ideographic pattern.

A Composite Sketch

In concluding the chapter we shall try to give a thumbnail sketch of the personality development of the Kibbutz-reared child.

The many similarities to the non-Kibbutz children will be disregarded here.

Compared with the child born in the ordinary family setting, the Kibbutz infant is immediately faced with a more difficult task, that of sorting out stimuli from, and coordinating responses to, more than one maternal figure. These frustrating demands upon the immature organism bring about a temporary withdrawal from the environment, and result in a slower tempo in intellectual growth and ego development. Once the hurdles during the first two or three years of life have been overcome, the acceleration in development is facilitated by a very benign environment and by the positive relationship with a number of giving adults, mother and metapelet included.

Mother, two metaplot (at least), father, the peers in the group, and biological siblings become highly cathected objects, but none figures singly, solely and exclusively. From the very beginning attachments and ambivalences are less intense than in the ordinary family situation. Early emotional independence and self-reliance are characteristic of the growing Kibbutz child. Relative independence of intense and complicated emotional involvement with parental figures remains characteristic of the adolescent and the young man of the Kibbutz. Adolescence itself is not so much of a *storm* and *stress* period; the child need not struggle for his independence and identity—he gained them long before. Intrapsychic conflict, at this and other periods, of the kind ultimately stemming from intrafamilial relationships is minimal. As a consequence, neurotic trends are relatively rare and insignificant.

A further consequence of the dispersal of cathexes is the less intense identification with any specific figure. Identification too is diffuse, and the resulting superego less threatening and punitive. There is an internalization of, and commitment to, social standards and ideology; there are feelings of guilt upon the violation of such standards. But, feelings of guilt are probably fewer and less intense.

Hostility of Kibbutz children is perhaps higher toward parental figures than toward peers and siblings. Its expression is apparently mitigated through self-control; more likely and more importantly, it is mitigated through sublimation and direction into communal and national goals. There is considerable sensitivity about hostility and aggression in interpersonal relationships, which are generally well conducted and harmonious.

Despite minimal sex role differentiation in Kibbutz child rearing and despite the diffuse identification, heterosexuality represents a major problem to Kibbutz adolescents. In view of the demands of Kibbutz ideology, expression of sexuality is suppressed. Kibbutz youngsters view premature sexuality as undesirable, but readily drop the defenses against it when there are no immediate social sanctions —or, of course, in marriage. Their defenses, generally, are more direct and less artful and complicated.

Although concerned about long-range social goals, the Kibbutz subject's own goals are rather short-range, characterized by a short future time perspective. This trend is primarily due to the fact that the Kibbutz does not hold out the freedom of vocational and occupational choice to its membership; individual goals of a longer range are determined by the collectivity. It may also be that the pessimism that tends to characterize our Kibbutz adolescents and young men does not permit them to get involved in long-range expectations.

This brief portrayal includes some of the main trends gleaned from our data. It is not our intent to pronounce value judgments upon the Kibbutz product. The facts are that Kibbutz child rearing was designed to raise new Kibbutz members, and is quite effective in doing so.

10.

Epilogue: Some Implications

To what extent do the results obtained suggest general principles concerning the relationship between child rearing and personality development? Are they applicable to societies other than the Kibbutz? The answer is that *some* generalizations and conclusions may prove useful beyond the boundaries of the society in which the investigation took place.

1. Multiple mothering, as it is practiced in the Kibbutz, despite some minor temporary difficulties and effects on the early developmental pattern, has no long-range deleterious effects upon personality development and character structure. American society (especially in the middle class) has become excessively sensitized to the posited "need" for close and continuous contacts between mother and child during infancy, popularized by Ribble and others, some three decades ago. Witness the great anxiety that many mothers experience even upon relatively brief separations from their children, although they may be left in the care and under supervision of competent substitutes. These mothers are often concerned about possible indelible marks that such "traumatic" separations may leave upon the personalities of their offspring. Similarly, many working mothers, as a result of their temporary absences from home and children, experience tremendous ambivalence, guilt and social pressure. This need for an exclusive dyadic relationship between

mother and infant has been highly overstated. Data such as those presented in this volume may help dispel the unnecessary anxiety and aid us in assuming a more balanced point of view regarding the issues involved.

2. The lesson of flexibility in personality development is to be emphasized. An excessive determinism with respect to early infancy has become the dominant attitude in the psychologically oriented professional and lay circles. The notion is that any untoward experience during infancy must have a crippling effect on personality forever. Little consideration is given to the autonomous ego functions, to secondary autonomy, and to the effects of corrective and therapeutic experiences embedded in the individual's environment. Little attention has also been paid to the differences in the developmental tempo and pattern of different egos or individuals. Too many predictions are being made following the examination of part of the pattern—the first part—rather than of a larger segment along the temporal dimension. Despite a slower early developmental tempo, the Kibbutz child surges forth subsequently under environmental conditions that are conducive to accelerated further growth and development. The pliability and plasticity of the human personality during the formative years, which extend way into adolescence, is hereby emphasized. Changes in pattern and changes in developmental trends and tempo, subsequent to the infantile period, need more emphasis and additional exploration.

3. The issues of what might be called "the dispersal of cathexes" has a considerable potential. The child in the ordinary family usually places all his eggs in the parental basket. His relationships with the parents are intense and, for a variety of reasons, negative as well as positive, i.e., ambivalent. Parental rejection is felt intensely; confused messages received from the parent ("double bind") are highly disturbing and disorganizing; excessive interdependence of a symbiotic nature is ego-stunting, etc. When the relationship with the parents is less intense, as it is for the Kibbutz child because of the comparative and comparable importance of the metaplot and the group, suffering and concomitant pathology are apparently obviated to a considerable extent. The child can readily turn to the other significant figures in his daily routine, if and when the inter-

action with a disturbed or neurotic parent is confusing, frustrating, anxiety provoking or debilitating.

As to the dispersal of the cathexes, the child can "take it," nay he might benefit from it. But could the parent in our society take it? Since parents are prone to encourage and perpetuate the emotional and economic dependency of their children upon them, the early introduction of several positive adult figures and children into the child's immediate environment might mitigate his intense emotional dependence and hasten the development of autonomy and independence as well as adequate emotional integration. Such a trend, however, would shake the covert parental emotional dependence upon their children and the related parental possessiveness which, if endangered, would threaten their narcissism to a marked extent.

4. Next there is the issue of identification with the parent. If we were to follow traditional theory, our predictions would be directed along two paths of pathological development. On the one hand, since the identification with the same-sex parent is not so intense, and since equality of the sexes in their social and occupational roles is stressed in collective education, the question may be raised whether there are strong trends of bisexuality or homosexuality in Kibbutz children. On the other hand, the diffuseness of identification and the lower intensity in the process experienced by Kibbutz children, may raise the question of inadequate superego development. In neither of these instances does the available evidence support the theoretical suppositions. The facts are that homosexuality among Kibbutz children is unknown. They seem to assume their sex roles in an unimpeded manner, quite adequately, as parents and as members of their society. Also, no serious defects in superego are noted. Kibbutz children are capable of experiencing guilt; they have obviously internalized moral standards and lose self-esteem if they do not behave according to them. However, their guilt feelings are not as strong as those of youngsters raised in the ordinary family; apparently the latter carry with them excess baggage of guilt resulting from unresolved intrafamilial relationships. Thus, the issue of identification (which is related to the one on the dispersal of cathexes) points up that the Kibbutz is by far less hazardous psychologically than many imagine. There is no need to be so much concerned, in our own

society, over the rapprochement between the roles of the sexes. Social and economic roles need not necessarily affect the sexual-biological role and the process of object choice in love relationships. Furthermore, the lower level and intensity of guilt, resulting from the dispersal of cathexes, which in turn reduces identification intensity, could liberate many individuals for more productive pursuits and ego-syntonic behavior.

5. The final point that may be made concerns the issue of group upbringing. The Kibbutz child is hardly ever alone. This lack of privacy is often bemoaned by outside observers. In this connection, Bettelheim's (1962) question is very much to the point: "Is it possible that the privatization of so much of modern middle-class life is not the consequence but rather the cause of human isolation from which modern man suffers and which the Kibbutz way of life has tried to counteract?" Although cathexes to parents, on the part of Kibbutz children, are less intense, cathexes to peers are more intense than in our own society. Moreover, cathexes to ideals in a new society and in a new and developing country seem to give meaning to life and fill the "existential vacuum" (Frankel, 1962) so omnipresent in the life of the individual in present-day industrialized Western society. A common goal, collective striving and group action give a sense of belongingness. The very structure of the Kibbutz society does not permit the isolation of the individual and the existential vacuum to become major phenomena. The future of relationships in our society need not inevitably be in the direction of further isolation and even "shallower cathexes" (Bellak, 1961) if we could find ways to expose our children rather early to meaningful group experiences and mutually satisfying contacts—directed by central goals and ideals. Admittedly, this is a big "if."

In considering the implications of Kibbutz child rearing for our own society, it must be pointed out that the Kibbutz product is not a paragon of stability, adjustment and happiness in the absolute sense. The aims of child rearing and education are, to a considerable extent, defined and determined by the society and culture in which the child grows up and for whose perpetuation he is preparing, or being prepared. We cannot transfer summarily, Kibbutz collective education into our own society. Its very structure is so different and necessarily inhospitable to such a venture. Some of the issues, discussed in this book may aid, however, in programmatic consideration and planning for the future. The implementation of some of the general ideas touched upon would require great effort and detailed careful development, but may be rewarded with an improvement in our "human condition."

References

Baratz, J. *A village by the Jordan.* New York: Roy Publishers, 1955.

Bayley, Nancy. On the growth of intelligence. *Amer. Psychologist,* 1955, *10,* 805-818.

Beck, S. J. *Rorschach's test.* Vol. I. New York: Grune & Stratton, 1950.

Beck, S. J. *The Rorschach experiment.* New York: Grune & Stratton, 1960.

Bellak, L. *The TAT and CAT in clinical use.* New York: Grune & Stratton, 1954.

Bellak, L. Personality structure in a changing world. *Arch. Gen. Psychiat.,* 1961, *5,* 183-185.

Beres, D., & Obers, S. J. The effects of extreme deprivation in infancy and psychic structure in adolescense: A study in ego development. In *The psychoanalytic study of the child.* Vol. V. New York: *International Univer. Press,* 1950, pp. 212-235.

Bettelheim, B. Does communal education work? *Commentary,* 1962, *33* 117-125.

Blum, G. S. A study of the psychoanalytic theory of psychosexua! development. *Genet. Psychol. Monogr.,* 1949, *39,* 3-99.

Blum, G. S. *The Blacky pictures* (manual of instructions). New York: Psychol. Corp., 1950.

Bowlby, J. *Maternal care and mental health.* Geneva: World Health Organization, 1951.

Caplan, G. Clinical observations on the emotional life of children in the communal settlements of Israel. In M. J. E. Senn (Ed.), *Prob-*

215

lems of infancy and childhood. New York: Josiah Macy, Jr. Foundation, 1954.

Davidson, Helen H. A measure of adjustment obtained from the Rorschach protocol. *J. proj. Tech.*, 1950, *14*, 31-38.

Doll, E. *Vineland Social Maturity Scale.* Minneapolis Minn.: Educational Test Bureau, 1946.

Doll, E. *The measurement of social competence: A manual for the Vineland Social Maturity Scale.* Minneapolis, Minn.: Educational Test Bureau, 1953.

Edwards, A. L. *Statistical analysis.* New York: Rinehart & Co., 1948.

Eisenstadt, S. N. Studies in social structure: I. Age groups and social structure—a comparison of some aspects of socialization in the cooperative and communal settlements of Israel. (Mimeo) Jerusalem, 1950.

Eisenstadt, S. N. *From generation to generation.* Glencoe, Ill.: The Free Press, 1956.

Eron, L. D. A normative study of the Thematic Apperception Test. *Psychol. Monogr.*, 1950, *64*, No. 9.

Fenichel, O. *The psychoanalytic theory of neurosis.* New York: W. W. Norton, 1945.

Forer, B. Word association and sentence completion methods. In A. I. Rabin & Mary R. Haworth (Eds.), *Projective techniques with children.* New York: Grune & Stratton, 1960.

Frankel. V. *Man's search for meaning: An introduction to logotherapy.* Boston: Beacon, 1962.

Freud, Anna, & Dann, Sophie. An experiment in group upbringing. In *The psychoanalytic study of the child*, Vol. VI. New York: International Univ. Press, 1951, pp. 127-169.

Golan, S. *Hachinuch Hameshutaf* (Collective Education). Merhavia, Israel: Sifriyat Poalim, 1961.

Goldfarb, W. Infant rearing and problem behavior. *Amer. J. Orthopsychiat.*, 1943a, *23*, 249-265.

Goldfarb, W. The effects of early institutional care on adolescent personality. *J. exp. Educ.*, 1943b, *12*, 106-129.

Goldfarb, W. Effects of early institutional care on adolescent personality: Rorschach data. *Amer. J. Orthopsychiat.*, 1944, *14*, 441-447.

Goldfarb, W. Infant rearing as a factor in foster home replacement. *Amer. J. Orthopsychiat.*, 1944, *14*, 162-166.

Goldfarb, W. Variations in adolescent adjustment of institutionally-reared children. *Amer. J. Orthopsychiat.*, 1947, *17*, 449-457.

Goldfarb, W. Emotional and intellectual consequences of psychologic deprivation in infancy: a revaluation. In P. Hoch & J. Zubin (Eds.), *Psychopathology of childhood*. New York: Grune & Stratton, 1955.

Goodenough, Florence. *Measurement of intelligence by drawings*. New York: World Book Co., 1926.

Goodenough, Florence, & Harris, D. B. Studies in the psychology of children's drawings: II 1928-1949, *Psychol. Bull.*, 1950, *47*, 369-433.

Griffiths, Ruth. *The abilities of babies*. New York: McGraw-Hill, 1954.

Hartmann, H. *Ego psychology and the problem of adaptation*. New York: International Univ. Press, 1958.

Henry, W. E. The thematic apperception technique in the study of culture-personality relations. *Genet. Psychol. Monogr.*, 1947, *35*, 3-135.

Henry, W. E. *The analysis of fantasy*. New York: John Wiley & Sons, 1956.

Herskovits, M. *Man and his works*. New York: Alfred A. Knopf, 1948.

Irvine, Elizabeth E. Observations on the aims and methods of child-rearing in communal settlements in Israel. *Human Relat.*, 1952 *V*, 247-275.

Kaffman, M. Evaluation of emotional disturbance in 403 Israel Kibbutz children. *Am. J. Psychiat.*, 1961, *117*, 732-738.

Kaplan, B. A study of Rorschach responses in four cultures. *Papers of the Peabody Museum*, 1954, XLII, *2*, 3-44.

Kardiner, A. The roads to suspicion, rage, apathy and societal disintegration. In I. Galdston, (Ed.), *Beyond the germ theory*. New York: Health Education Council, 1954.

Klopfer, B., Ainsworth, Mary D., Klopfer, W. G., & Holt, R. R. *Developments in the Rorschach technique*. New York: World Book Co., 1954.

Koestler, A. *Thieves in the night*. New York: MacMillan & Co., 1946.

Machover, Karen. *Personality projection in the drawing of the human figure*. Springfield, Ill.: Charles C. Thomas, 1949.

Murray, H. A. *Thematic Apperception Test manual*. Cambridge: Harvard Univer. Press, 1943.

Phillips, H. P. Problems of translation and meaning in field work. *Human Org.*, Winter 1959-1960, *18*, 184-192.

Pine, F. A manual for rating drive content in the Thematic Apperception Test. *J. proj. Tech.*, 1960, *24*, 32-45.

Rabin, A. I. The Israeli Kibbutz (collective settlement) as a "laboratory" for testing psychodynamic hypotheses. *Psychol. Rec.,* 1957a, *7,* 111-115.

Rabin, A. I. Personality maturity of Kibbutz (Israeli Collective Settlement) and non-Kibbutz children as reflected in Rorschach findings. *J. proj. Tech.,* 1957b, *21,* 148-153.

Rabin, A. I. Infants and children under conditions of "intermittent" mothering in the Kibbutz. *Amer. J. Orthopsychiat.,* 1958a, *XXVIII,* 577-584.

Rabin, A. I. Some psychosexual differences between Kibbutz and non-Kibbutz Israeli boys. *J. proj. Tech.,* 1958b, *22,* 328-332.

Rabin, A. I. Attitudes of Kibbutz children to family and parents. *Amer. J. Orthopsychiat.,* 1959, *XXIX,* 172-179.

Rabin, A. I. Kibbutz adolescents. *Am. J. Orthopsychiat.,* 1961a, *31,* 493-504.

Rabin, A. I. Personality study in Israeli Kibbutzim. In B. Kaplan (Ed)., *Studying personality cross-culturally.* Evanston, Ill.: Row, Peterson, 1961b.

Rabin, A. I., & Limuaco, Josefina A. Sexual differentiation of American and Filipino children as reflected in the draw-a-person test. *J. soc. Psychol.,* 1959, *50,* 207-211.

Rohde, Armander R. *The sentence completion method.* New York: Ronald Press, 1957.

Rosenzweig, S., & Fleming, Edith. Apperceptive norms for the Thematic Apperception Test. II. An empirical investigation. *J. Pers.,* 1949, *17,* 483-503.

Rotter, J. B. Word association and sentence completion methods. In H. H. Anderson, & Gladys L. Anderson, (Eds.), *An introduction to projective techniques.* Chapter 9, pp. 279-311. New York: Prentice Hall, 1951.

Sacks, J. M., & Levy, S. The sentence completion test. In L. E. Abt & L. Bellak (Eds.), *Projective psychology,* New York: Knopf, 1950.

Schafer, R. *Psychoanalytic interpretation in Rorschach testing.* New York: Grune & Stratton, 1954.

Siegel, S. *Nonparametric statistics.* New York: McGraw Hill, 1956.

Spiro, M. E. Is the family universal? *Amer. Anthropologist,* 1954, *56,* 839-846.

REFERENCES

Spiro, M. E. *Children of the Kibbutz.* Cambridge, Mass.: Harvard Univer. Press, 1958.

Spitz, R. Unhappy and fatal outcomes of emotional deprivation and stress in infancy. In I. Galdson (Ed.), *Beyond the germ theory,* 1954.

Swenson, C. H. Sexual differentiation on the Draw-a-person test. *J. clin. Psychol.,* 1955, *11*, 37-40.

Wallace, M., & Rabin, A. I. Temporal experience. *Psychol. Bull.,* 1960, *57*, 213-236.

Wittenborn, J. R. Some Thematic Apperception Test norms and a note on the use of test cards in guidance of college students. *J. clin. Psychol.,* 1949, *5*, 157-161.

Yarrow, L. J. Maternal deprivation toward an empirical and conceptual re-evaluation. *Psychol. Bull.,* 1961, 459-490.

Zohar, Z (Ed.). Hachinneh Hameshutaf (Collective education). Merhavia, Israel: Sifriat Poalim, 1947.

Index